MW00852615

PRAISE FOR *A TOUCH OF THE MADNESS*

"There can be only one . . . Larry Kasanoff! He is right, embrace the crazy to be more creative. I love *A Touch of the Madness*!"

—CHRISTOPHER LAMBERT, "THE HIGHLANDER"

"E! has been reporting on Kasanoff and his movies for years, but we never got the real behind the scenes scoop—the literal method to his madness of creativity—until now. It's a fun, helpful read!"

—LARRY NAMER, FOUNDER OF E! ENTERTAINMENT

"I loved and laughed at how Larry has navigated the choppy waters of Hollywood with *A Touch of the Madness*, and took away a whole new perspective on innovation. It inspired me to embrace the madness!"

—CAPTAIN SANDY YAWN, STAR OF BRAVO'S *BELOW DECK MEDITERRANEAN*

"*A Touch of the Madness* has no charts, no graphs, no PowerPoint presentations, just a wealth of entertaining and eccentric stories that can reframe how you think about innovation for your business."

—MARTY POMPADUR, FORMER CHAIRMAN OF NEWS CORPORATION (EUROPE)

"I wish I could prescribe *A Touch of the Madness*—it will change the way you think about creativity, with the only side effect being you're having more fun; I recommend taking this as often as needed."

—BLAISE AGUIRRE, MD, ASSOCIATE PROFESSOR AT PSYCHIATRY HARVARD MEDICAL SCHOOL

"Don't miss this hilarious tour of the secret underbelly of Hollywood! Larry Kasanoff's signature approach to getting things done is wild, magical and ultimately meaningful."

—PAMELA MEYER, AUTHOR OF *LIESPOTTING*

A TOUCH OF
THE MADNESS

A TOUCH OF THE MADNESS

*How to Be More Innovative
in Work and Life . . .
by Being a Little Crazy*

LAWRENCE KASANOFF

BenBella Books, Inc.
Dallas, TX

The events, locations, and conversations in this book, while true, are re-created from the author's memory. However, the essence of the story, and the feelings and emotions evoked, are intended to be accurate representations. In certain instances, names, persons, organizations, and places have been changed to protect an individual's privacy.

BenBella Books, Inc.
10440 N. Central Expressway
Suite 800
Dallas, TX 75231
benbellabooks.com
Send feedback to feedback@benbellabooks.com

BenBella is a federally registered trademark.

Printed in the United States of America
10 9 8 7 6 5 4 3 2 1

Library of Congress Control Number: 2023003571
ISBN 9781637744239 (hardcover)
ISBN 9781637744246 (electronic)

Editing by Scott Calamar
Proofreading by Isabelle Rubio and Sarah Vostock
Text design and composition by Aaron Edmiston
Cover design by Brigid Pearson
Cover image © iStock / Mark Tomaras (barrel); © Shutterstock / fluke samed (fire)
Printed by LakeBook Manufacturing

For all the great scoundrels . . .

CONTENTS

The Madness And Mindfulness
Thay In Thailand

Chapter One

WELCOME TO THE MADNESS

I wanted to be a movie producer since I was a little kid, and I got lucky and became head of production of an independent film studio called Vestron when I was right out of grad school.

By the way, I thought I nailed getting this job because I was such hot stuff having just graduated with my MBA from Wharton. That lasted about five minutes, until my boss in his welcoming speech my first day said, "By the way, if you pull any of that business school crap, you're fired."

So much for the Ivy League in Hollywood.

OK, back to the story. Vestron rode the boom in home video, which at the time was relatively new and exploding. We were sort of the Netflix of the day. I had to deliver eighty movies a year: buy 'em, produce 'em, cofinance 'em—doesn't matter, said my boss, but eighty movies a year and don't lose money on any of them. So mostly we made action movies, comedies, horror films, and fun commercial stuff.

Then along came this movie called *Platoon*, and I wanted to make it. This was not at all our kind of film. The people in it became stars, but most weren't stars at the time. The director, Oliver Stone, had done only one prior movie (which we cofinanced), and while I thought it was brilliant, it didn't do much business.

Platoon wasn't a catchy title. It dealt with the extraordinarily serious topic of the Vietnam War and how it affected the kids who went. The tagline was: "The first casualty of war is innocence." It was not the kind of movie we were making.

To his incredible credit, my boss, Austin Furst—who was a talented, disruptive entrepreneur—said, "OK, you are the head of production; if you want to do it, you can do it."

But there was a "but."

"You have to bet your job," he warned. "If it fails, you're fired." He wasn't bluffing—he fired people all the time.

"What do you want to do?"

I took the shot.

Much later, I saw the movie one early morning at a film festival in Italy, right after it had been finished.

I am probably the only person in the world who giggled their entire way through *Platoon*, not because it wasn't amazing, but because the whole time I was thinking, *Thank God, I'm not getting fired!*

Platoon went on to win Best Picture that year at the Academy Awards.

A few months later, I ran into Oliver Stone, the director, at a bar in New York City. "You know, kid," he said, "I always liked you. You have a touch of the madness."

A touch of the madness? I thought. Is he saying I am a bit crazy? Was I crazy?

I had to think about that. Then I realized:

My boss encouraged a touch of the madness by letting a twenty-five-year-old run a huge production slate and take a risk on a movie no one else would touch. I had a touch of the madness by betting a once-in-a-lifetime job to do it. The director had a touch of the madness by never giving up his battle to make a Vietnam movie in a way no one ever had.

The whole innovation that was *Platoon* would not have happened without a touch of the madness.

I realized I loved that phrase. It hit me: innovation demands a touch of the madness.

First, why does everyone talk about innovation? Why is it so important?

The current of the river of life will always try to pull you towards the middle, towards complacency and mediocrity. This is true for every person and every company. It's a problem because other companies that don't give in to that current will eclipse you.

Companies and organizations tend to be comfortable with the tried and true. But the audience, i.e., your customers, are attracted to what's new, different, and better.

The best tool you have for swimming against that current of mediocrity is innovation. To grow and become a great company, a great entrepreneur, you must actively embrace it. You can become pretty good without it, but not great. You must take a shot.

And to be very innovative, you have to be a bit crazy. You need a touch of the madness.

That's what I foster in myself, in my company, and in my movies. It's what companies have to cultivate in their culture, their employees. You can't be great without it.

And it doesn't mean to just be a little crazy in what you think up; it also means you must have a mad enthusiasm, a crazy sense of purpose and devotion and perseverance. A touch of the madness in how you create it, implement it, and make it thrive.

How to do it? Three steps:

CREATE—*Find the Essence*

ASK—*Anybody Anywhere for Anything You Want*

PLAY—*It All Like a Game*

Chapter Two

CREATE

First, create a great idea with a touch of the madness. Simple, right?

A touch of the madness gives you some guidelines for how to be more creative and innovative. They are:

- Find the essence of your idea.
- Know your target customer/audience.
- Let technology serve your idea, not the other way around.
- Once you have created your idea, never let go.

And do it all with a mad fire in your belly, never-give-up mindset.

Here is the breakdown of the four steps.

ESSENCE OF AN IDEA

When I decided to make *Mortal Kombat* into a movie, everyone told me I was crazy, and my career would be over. "You can't make video games into movies," and every prior attempt had failed. It had never been done successfully at that point.

The Secret To Mortal Kombat

But here is a secret. I never thought I was making a video game into a movie. I thought I was making the essence of that video game—the thing that made it so successful—into a movie.

Think of a game or intellectual property as a pyramid. The game to me was not the apex of the intellectual property pyramid. It was one rung down. The apex is the magic pixie dust that made *Mortal Kombat* such a great video game.

I have always thought with *Mortal Kombat* it was empowerment, wrapped in a visually stunning package, of course, but empowerment nonetheless. Martial arts teaches that you don't have to be the biggest and the strongest to win, if you focus, study, and do the right thing. And the game really reinforces that.

When wandering around an old-fashioned arcade (this was a place in the old days where you went to play games that were in freestanding, big, console machines), trying to decide if I should bet my career on *Mortal Kombat*, an eleven-year-old kid slapped a quarter down on the arcade game, looked up at me, and said, "I challenge YOU to *Mortal Kombat*."

Then, he beat the hell out of me. And the game egged him on, saying things in that great, deep, resonant *Mortal Kombat* voice like, "Sub-Zero Wins! Flawless victory. You lose!"

The kid left feeling great. I decided then and there to go for it.

Now, once you have that essence, that top view, you can decide where to sprinkle it. Recently, I was executive producer of a hit *Mortal Kombat* movie—it was my nineteenth *Mortal Kombat* production in twenty-something years. I have produced it in every medium in the world. The franchise has grossed almost $10 billion.

Here's another one.

Several years ago, I went to Lego to try to get the rights to make a full-length animated film. Lego had not done that before. They were concerned that if it didn't work, it might embarrass them. So we all decided to make a movie that would go straight to DVD. If it hit, great, and we could go make a bigger one next. If it failed, it would be under the radar and no one would really notice.

I raised independent money to make the movie and set a deal with Universal to distribute it.

Now, what is the essence of Lego? This one was easy for us because Lego knew. The essence was "we build on each other." Lego, when the characters came to life, was not just about blocks and bricks or kids playing, it was about teamwork, and counting on each other, and well, building on each other.

We put that into the first full-length Lego feature film, *Lego: The Adventures of Clutch Powers*. It was a DVD hit. We wound up doing *Lego Star Wars: The Empire Strikes Out*, Lego theme park rides, and more. All with that essence infused into it.

In my opinion, Lego's success is not a fluke—they know their essence.

Know the essence of your idea—what makes it so appealing and great?

OK, next step to creating great ideas . . .

AUDIENCE

Who do you work for?

Your boss, your foreman, your editor, your board?

No, you work for your audience. For your customers. That is a huge responsibility.

DIRTY DANCING—*"THAT'S THE POINT, YOU IDIOT!"*

When we started *Dirty Dancing*, and Jennifer Grey was brought up to star, I—thirty seconds into the movie business at that point—suggested maybe we needed someone more famous, more glamorous. She was a wonderful actress, but an "everywoman," I said.

"That is the point, you idiot," said the movie's real godfather, and my current business partner, Jimmy Ienner. "Every woman in the world will identify with her and think they too will get a good-looking bad boy to become a good boy for them. That is your audience." He was right, of course.

KANO AND THE KID

Here is another example. In *Terminator 2*, Arnold Schwarzenegger's character—the Terminator—gets half of the skin on his face blown off, revealing his metal exoskeleton beneath.

In *Mortal Kombat* lives a character called Kano, who also has part of his face missing, revealing a metal plate with a LED kind of eye.

They looked a bit similar to me, and since I made both movies relatively close to each other, I decided I would redesign Kano as we migrated the characters from the game to the first live-action *Mortal Kombat* movie.

Close to that time, as a favor to someone, we had a class of kids from a junior high school in to see how we build sets and design movies. I was showing them around.

Fight rehearsal—they loved it.

Goro the eight-foot-tall animatronic creature—they loved it.

Wild statues and weapons from the parallel realm of Outworld—they loved it.

Character designs for the movie—they loved—wait, hold on.

When we came to the designs for Kano, one boy started breathing heavily.

"Is that Kano?" he asked, nervously.

"Yup!" I said proudly.

"But Kano has a metallic eye," he said, now out of breath. I started to worry a bit about the kid. Maybe he was sick.

I explained I didn't want Kano to look in *Mortal Kombat* anything like Arnold in *Terminator* 2 and—

He interrupted. He began to hyperventilate.

"Kano has a metallic eye patch. You can't change that."

"But—"

"Kano has a metallic eye patch." He was sweating, breathing quick and shallow. He was in the throes of a full-blown panic attack.

All because I was going to change Kano's metallic eye.

My mistake hit me. My audience point-blank told me what to do.

"OK, OK," I said, "you are right. Kano does have a metallic eye patch. We will change it back." I ripped the design off the board and tore it up.

Immediately, he started to calm down. He made me promise again, and then he was fine.

What I realized so suddenly was that I wanted to change Kano because I wanted to do something a bit different so I didn't repeat myself, and so I would be creatively challenged every second. But see what is wrong with the previous sentence? It is all "I" and not "my audience."

The audience, embodied by that poor kid, couldn't care less about what I wanted—and nor should they care. They wanted their beloved character to look in the movies as he does in the game.

We changed Kano back that day, and he remains a popular character in the movies and games, twenty-five years later.

MAD SCIENTISTS IN JAPAN

We financed at Vestron a campy horror comedy called *Reanimator*, based on an H. P. Lovecraft novel. It parodied '50s horror movies.

The movie featured a mad scientist trying to reanimate, or bring back from the dead, people.

It was wild, crazy, over-the-top, full of gratuitous violence and goofy sex. People loved it, and it became a huge hit.

The scene everyone talked about most was this: towards the end, the mad scientist has the damsel in distress, wearing very little, strapped down to an operating table in his mad scientist lab.

Oh, and his head has been cut off, so he carries it around gripped by the hair in his right hand. Naturally.

At one point, the headless scientist stands next to the damsel and, holding his head, "kisses" her on the cheek, then neck, then his hand and the head goes down out of frame and well, you get the picture.

It became known—and forgive this if you are prudish—as the "head giving head" scene. Again, talked about in the US and in Europe, but nothing more.

In Japan, a different story. Our chief of the Japanese office had other plans. He put the "head giving head" scene on the video box. He made posters he sent to every video store in the country. (Remember, you couldn't actually see any nudity or anything, it was all implied, and more ridiculous than sexy.) And he took out ads and billboards.

The "head giving head" scene became a phenomenon in Japan. And the video became one of the biggest in Japanese history.

Why? Because our chief of Japan knew his audience. The Japanese read wild manga and watch over-the-top crazy (to us) anime. Our chief embraced this and was not afraid. Nor should he have been. He came to New York, proudly, to celebrate with us and give everyone their own "head giving head" posters.

Know your audience and act, boldly, on that knowledge.

I have a little speech before we start every movie: "You don't work for me, the director, or the studio," I say, "you work for the audience, your customers."

You have to know them—not just impersonal demographic info, but what they really want.

IDEAS DRIVE TECH

Let your idea drive your technology, not the other way around. See the Eiffel Tower in your mind, then figure out how to build it, versus seeing lots of metal joints and figuring out an idea for them.

This is where things like the metaverse come into play. The metaverse, for example, doesn't really exist yet, as I write this. The question is, should it exist—for you?! Only if you have a great idea that the metaverse will help you bring to your audience.

STAR TREK *VS. THE STUDIO*

We also produce theme park rides. A while ago, we wanted to make one where the audience, seeing in stereoscopic 3D, could walk through a *Star Trek* Borg cube floating in space (if you are not up on *Star Trek*, the Borg are chief bad guys).

The problem: At that point, there were no cameras that could move and shoot 3D at the same time. 3D was all stationary. But so what? It would make for a great experience. We pitched it, sold it, and THEN, with another company, set out to invent a 3D moving camera, called a Steadicam.

We succeeded, which helped drive the craze of 3D movies.

Then one of the studios came to us, saying they were going to start a 3D TV network, and could we provide content?

"Sure," we said. "What kind of content do you want?"

"We don't know."

"OK, who is your audience?" we asked.

"We don't know."

Finally, we asked, "Why are you doing this?"

They answered, "Because everyone else is. It's the hot tech thing."

Their network lasted maybe six months.

Ideas rule; technology helps them come alive. Chasing the new hot thing will get you nowhere. Creating a new idea and then using whatever means you need to make it work will succeed.

HOLD ON TO YOUR IDEA; NEVER LET IT GO

Once you have gone through these first three steps, and now have your great idea, there is one more step. Hold on for dear life. Never give up. Everyone—like the current of that river I mentioned—will try to dissuade you. Do not let them. Be bold and big if you'd like, but once you lock on, never lose focus. Just do not give up on it.

This is really the most important step, because talent—a great idea—is only half the battle. This is the other half.

YOU GOTTA SEE THESE

At that same first job, Vestron, where we made *Platoon*, one of the filmmakers we backed—let's call him Ernest—had the greatest ideas for horror movies. We would often green-light low-budget movies in those days just based on the concept, or the poster, so to speak.

The only problem with Ernest is that he would always go over budget, and then "rob Peter to pay Paul." In other words, he would use down payments on movies #2, #3, and #4 to finish his over-budget movie #1. Or maybe he was stealing the money?

We didn't really care too much in a sense because all those movies were wildly profitable, even with the constant "over-budgets."

But at a point, things got worse, kind of unignorable.

My boss, Austin, and I confronted him in a suite in Cannes at the film market. Austin, a great guy but one who could be really intimidating when he wanted, paced up and down, yelling at Ernest, "How could you do this to us? We trusted you. We believed in you!"

Ernest just sat there, implacable, legs crossed, one arm draped over the back of the couch. Almost smiling.

Austin turned things up a notch. "We financed you, turned you into a mini studio, and this is how you repay us?"

No response. Calm as can be.

"We have a lien on your business, your house. We can take everything and bankrupt you." This went on for twenty minutes.

Austin, finally, asked: "What have you got to say for yourself?"

Ernest smiled and said, "Austin, Larry, I completely understand where you are coming from. But before I address that, please let me show you something."

And he lifted the arm draped over the couch to reveal he was holding three movie posters—for NEW movies.

"I wanted to show you these concepts for three new films."

In the face of losing everything he had, his entire plan was three NEW IDEAS. That was it.

"You gotta see these concepts!"

And you know what? They were great. So you know what we did?

We bought all three movies.

Even though he had either stolen or been wildly irresponsible with our money, the ideas were so good, we went for it. And they all wound up making money.

He had such faith in his ideas, that even though we could have taken his house, he was unwavering, focused, determined, and would do anything to get these movies made. He truly believed in them.

By the way, our focus, our great idea, was to find these filmmakers with a touch of the madness and take chances to keep our supply of films robust and innovative. And it worked.

"TIME OF MY LIFE" ALMOST WASN'T

Here is another example. *Dirty Dancing* was a script in turnaround, meaning another studio had developed it, but then deeming it no good, put in on the shelf. We bought it from them. No one wanted to make it.

And it was in trouble.

Long story how, but our company managed to lure a music and producing legend, who lived nearby, named Jimmy Ienner, to come oversee it. Jimmy then brought in a music supervisor named Michael Lloyd.

The song "Time of My Life" was originally done as a high falsetto. No good, Jimmy and Michael knew. They tried and tried to get someone to sing it low and deep, but no one wanted to. They finally convinced Bill Medley of the Righteous Brothers to do it, I think as a favor.

He recorded it in one afternoon. Now we had our low and deep version.

But his manager didn't like it. Demanded all kinds of changes. No one else liked it either. Everyone—the record company, our director—wanted changes.

Jimmy and Michael said, "Sure. We will change it."

Two weeks later, they sent in the song with a new date on it, and a note saying, "Here is the latest version. And we have sent it to radio stations, who like it. Hope you like it as well."

Everyone—the manager, the director—all loved the new changes. The changes were brilliant, they said, just the thing.

But you know what Jimmy and Michael really changed?

Nothing.

Not a note.

They just put a new date on the label. That's all they changed. The date.

Jimmy and Michael knew what they had. They believed in their idea. In the face of constant criticism, they sent it to even more people (the radio stations). They doubled down and went bigger.

And the song is one of the most successful in history. It won the Academy Award and the Grammy that year for Best Song. Jimmy is my partner in my company to this day, and Michael is still our music supervisor and great friend.

FIRST THEY GREET YOU, THEN THEY EAT YOU

When making low-budget horror movies at Vestron, I would often green-light them, as I've said, just by the poster—the concept. But what if the poster is fantastic, but the movie, not so much?

That's the decision facing me on a movie called, no kidding, *Blood Diner*. The creator/director, Jackie Kong, I really liked. She was a whirlwind force of nature. Talk about a touch of the madness! (I mean that, of course, as a compliment.) She certainly swam away from the current of the river of life and avoided the middle.

The concept was fun, and Jackie was the kind of extreme talent I liked to back, but I didn't think the script was good enough. Even so, we ordered the poster concepts.

I still remember seeing the poster for the first time. It featured a beautiful almost art deco shot of an old American diner at night, with the tagline:

First they greet you, then they eat you.

I just loved it. I knew that alone would sell a million videocassettes. But could I green-light this? It was way, way out there.

I thought this poster and tagline were so good, I had a feeling I would somehow years from then be glad I did.

So I green-lit the movie.

It was, well, out there. Bizarre. I didn't really understand the film as I didn't comprehend the script, but it did sell a gazillion cassettes, and then I lost track of it.

A few years ago, I started getting calls to do interviews for *Blood Diner*. I thought someone was punking me.

Then I got invited to come to its weekend showing at Quentin Tarantino's theater in LA.

No way, I thought. This film is still showing in theaters? Decades later?

I cajoled two of my wildest, up-for-anything DJ sister friends to come with me. I wore a baseball cap, high collar—like a cartoon character trying not to be recognized.

The midnight show was—sold out! So crowded I couldn't even find seats with my friends.

Now, I can't say even all these years later I really understand the appeal, but as I've said in this book, who cares what I think—the audience absolutely loved it!

I learned *Blood Diner* has become a cult classic. My feeling years ago that in the future I would be glad I green-lit the movie came true.

All because of a great poster and tagline. That simple idea became responsible for a movie that has been playing for over thirty years.

OK, so first, create your ideas, but then let them be your North Star. Believe in them.

Chapter Three

ASK

N ow you have created your great idea and your unwavering faith in it. What's next?

Second way to cultivate a touch of the madness: ASK.

ASK for what you want.

ASK ANYBODY for ANYTHING you want, ANYWHERE.

The easiest way to get anything you want is to ASK. Call anybody; ask for anything in pursuit of your goals. No such thing as being shy. "No" is just the beginning.

ASK ASK ASK

If you could call anyone in the world, and ask them one question, who would you call and what would you ask? Right now, answer!

Most people can't. Don't feel bad. They don't know. That is because they don't assume they could call anyone in the world. Well, you can. Here are some examples.

GUNS N' ROSES: YOU COULD BE MINE—IF YOU WILL JUST . . .

When we were making *Terminator* 2, it was at the time the most expensive movie ever produced. Of course, we wanted to make sure every base, every promotional opportunity, was covered.

In those days, MTV played music videos and was a huge phenomenon. A video on MTV, if a hit, could be played like fifteen times a day, for free.

So I wanted to do a music video for *T*2. First, I asked the studio. They said no. Remember, no is just the beginning.

I asked the director—he was all for it as long as it was natural to the movie.

I asked Arnold—who was not contractually obligated to do this—he said sure, if you get the biggest band in the world. I said no prob, who do you think that is? He called his brother-in-law, who was in the music business, listened, then turned to me, and said, "Guns N' Roses."

I said sure.

I didn't know anyone involved with Guns N' Roses.

I called Geffen Records, the band's management, and their A&R team. The band was about to put out a two-album set called *Use Your Illusion*, destined to be the biggest album of the year.

We invited them to come see a private rough-cut screening of the movie.

The band liked it.

They asked us which song we wanted to use. We picked one called "You Could Be Mine." Axl Rose, the band's lead singer, told me it was exactly the one he would have chosen, so we were in sync. Honestly, a lucky break, but we did ask.

Great song, but it wasn't going to be the first single released, the one that would get all the promotion. We needed it to be. (In those days of albums, the record company would pick one song that they would release to radio stations to promote the album, and then if the audience wanted to buy that song, they had to buy the whole album.)

We asked Arnold and his then wife, Maria, if they would host a dinner party for Guns N' Roses. Gracious as can be, they did. I pitched the band the idea of switching singles—changing the whole release pattern of the album. They didn't say yes or no, but they seemed to like the dinner conversation and the plan. Especially Slash, their lead guitarist.

The next day, I went to present that to Geffen Records. It was like twenty of them and me.

You have to understand, this was the absolute biggest, hottest band in the world, poised to release the biggest album of the year, and I was asking them to switch singles, which means change their entire marketing strategy. Now, their being associated with *T*2 could be great for them, but *T*2 hadn't come out yet, so it was a gamble.

One of their executives really let me have it. "You movie guys think you can just waltz in here and get us to change our strategy for our carefully crafted release of the biggest band in the world and we'll just do it. Let me tell you something—"

Then Slash walked in. He saw me, smiled, and pointed to me. He said, "Hey, the movie guy. Let's do what he wants."

They all jumped up and said, "Yes, of course, Slash; wonderful idea; we were just about to do that, Slash; let's do it."

Now we had the director, star, band, and record company all on board. You know what we didn't have?

The money. Remember, the studio at first said no. I did all this without having the money!

But with everyone on board and our song being the new single, I gambled they couldn't really say no anymore. I asked again and they said yes.

No is only the beginning.

But it wasn't over because we had to actually make the video. In the concept of the video, the Terminator is hunting Guns N' Roses to kill them, but when he sees Axl Rose, the band's lead, his Terminator vision says "WASTE OF AMMO," they nod to each other, and he lets them go.

We used footage from the movie, cut with new footage we shot for the video. A big part of that is the band playing a concert at what is supposed to be an LA landmark venue of rock 'n' roll called the Roxy. But as opposed to re-creating the Roxy somewhere private—a set—the band would, for authenticity's sake, only shoot the exteriors at the real Roxy.

The problem is the real Roxy is on Sunset Boulevard, the main street in the middle of Hollywood. It meant, of course, as soon as we put up a sign on Sunset Boulevard on the Roxy marquee, which we needed for the shot in the video, saying "TONIGHT ONLY: GUNS N' ROSES IN CONCERT," the world would think it was true and start a mini riot.

I had to ask everyone—studio, police, Arnold—if we could do that.

They agreed, and it did sort of start a mini riot—a friendly one, but huge. There were dozens of police cars. The band, as I recall, was a bit late, because even they couldn't get through the crowd. Arnold waited for them with his usual class and aplomb.

It goes on and on.

At the end of the day, the song went platinum, the video did play fifteen times a day on MTV, and it won a video of the year fan contest on MTV.

WHY?

Because I never stopped asking.

TRUE LIES: *TRUE REQUEST*

The story of the movie *True Lies* is based on a French film called *La Totale!* Everything came together: Arnold wanted to star; Jim Cameron was going to direct it; and the money would be there. But the only thing we didn't have were the rights.

The rights to remake *La Totale!* were held by a producer who was much older and more accomplished than me at the time.

Nevertheless, I called him and said, "We want to use this story as a vehicle for all these wonderful people who would really be grateful if you give us the rights, so will you?"

Crazy, right?

But he did and we made the movie.

Ask.

BOBBLEHEAD CHER

Not too long ago, we had Cher in an animated movie, using her voice but also her likeness, playing Bobble-head Cher.

When doing press for the movie, Cher was asked by *People* magazine, "You've never done an animated movie before. Why did you pick this one?"

Cher's answer: "No one ever asked me before."

I asked her.

If Cher, one of the most famous and iconic people in the world, never was asked to be in an animated movie, can you imagine who else is out there, waiting for you to call and ask them something!? Don't assume you can't get them because they are too big or a million people must have asked before. You never know.

Ask.

TWO ARRESTED; THIRD INVESTED

What do you do when asking seems to be going nowhere, when you are tired and running out of juice to ask even one more time?

Ask again.

We were raising money for a movie. One of our agents brought in a Korean agent friend of his, who was somehow an agent/priest. I never really understood that, but the agent we knew vouched for him.

The agent/priest, let's call him Father Evan, brought in a Korean investor to our studio in Santa Monica. It went great! The investor agreed to the deal during the meeting.

We popped champagne, toasted with him, took pictures all around.

The investor was to fly back to Korea and wire the money right away.

He did fly back to Korea—but was promptly arrested on the tarmac when he got there. Put in handcuffs. We saw it on the news.

Quite disappointing, of course. We certainly did not see that one coming.

Father Evan rushed over. "Not to worry," he said. "Slight setback—I've got another investor."

A week later he brought in another investor. We were more cautious and asked many more questions this time.

Once again, the investor agreed. We congratulated each other, but being a bit more reserved, no champagne this time. Still, pictures all around again.

Investor #2 flew back to Korea. Landed. No police. Whew!

But we "whewed" too soon. Two weeks later, he was arrested for fraud.

Now, we weren't going to even listen when Father Evan told us once more: "No problem, it happens." We weren't even going to let him bring—you guessed it—a third investor. But the agent who introduced us to Father Evan was a longtime friend and cajoled us to try once more.

When investor #3 came in, we did muster up the energy to ask one more time. But that's virtually all we did. We hardly showed him around our studio.

We were so reserved, it seemed like we really didn't need the money. It was, in reality, because we no longer had confidence any of Father Evan's clients would come through, let alone avoid jail.

Investor #3 saw our nonchalant attitude as a sign of strength, figuring lots of people must want the deal if we were so casual about it.

He wired us the money (it was several million dollars) the next day.

Always ask, then ask again. You never know.

YOU CAN'T HURRY LOVE

What to do when the person you are asking is your friend?

At Vestron I made a comedy film about a guy who moves to LA and joins a dating service. It was the first film under a long-term pact with a talent management company that represented John Travolta, among others.

The deal was: for each movie they would provide a certain number of famous people to be in it.

For *You Can't Hurry Love*, they had to put three celebrities in the movie. They had Sally Kellerman, one of the stars of *M*A*S*H*, a brilliant seventies comedy, and Kristy McNichol, from the film *Little Darlings* and the TV show *Empty Nest*; both big in those days.

They needed a third.

The brain of funny writer/director Richard Martini hatched *You Can't Hurry Love*. It was really his baby.

He targeted for his third celebrity Charles Grodin, star of *The Heartbreak Kid*, *Catch*-22, and, later, *Beethoven*, and his own talk show. I think he was one of the funniest people on earth. Anything he said, he made sound hysterical.

Richard and Chuck Grodin knew each other via a mutual friend, so Richard sent the script and asked him to do it.

Chuck called Richard and said he couldn't, as he was shooting another movie (*The Couch Trip*) the same day. What could Richard do? Chuck said he was sorry.

The next day, Richard's phone rang. Charles Grodin.

"Are you asking me to do this as a friend, as a favor?" asked Chuck.

"Well, yeah, if you say yes, Larry green-lights the film," replied Richard.

"OK, I will be there," Chuck said.

We green-lit the movie. On Chuck's shooting day, we had a car and driver waiting at Chuck's other set. When that film broke for lunch, Chuck hopped in the car and sped over to ours. He didn't even tell the other film, which in itself was a touch of the madness. Crazy to do that on a film.

He nailed our scene in like an hour and rushed back to his set, where they were none the wiser.

It's a highlight of the movie, which did well.

A few years later, Chuck started his own talk show. He called Richard to ask him to come shoot comedy segments for the show. Richard said he couldn't—a contract to write another movie took up all his current time. He said he was sorry.

What could Chuck do?

The next day, Chuck's phone rang. Richard Martini.

"Are you asking me to do this as a favor, as a friend?" asked Richard.

"Well, yeah, I need you to help my new show."

Richard said, "I will be there tomorrow," and worked doing comedy segments for Chuck's show for six months.

Friendship is tough to define in business. I find there used to be more of it. But if you live by that code, delivering for your actual friends and being able to count on them when they really need you, it is wonderful. I recommend giving it a try.

A 10 *IN ITALY*

What do you do when you have maybe five seconds to decide whether to ask or not?

One of my early assignments at Vestron: go meet John and Bo Derek and make a sequel to the movie 10. That film, featuring Bo Derek, became a sensation in the eighties and catapulted Bo into sex symbol superstardom. John had been a huge movie star in the fifties and sixties, appearing in films including *The Ten Commandments*.

Bo graced the cover of every major magazine in the world, often more than once. She held the record for *Playboy* covers (five), for example. But the press also targeted the couple relentlessly because John was thirty years older, and while Bo always said she was with him for love and stayed with him until literally the day he died, the press just ate up the age difference angle.

Any way you slice it, though, they always got tons of press. All this press, of course, we figured, could be great for a sequel movie because no matter what, it would attract a lot of attention.

The first time I met Bo and John, in our offices in LA, they struck me as literally the best-looking people I had ever seen. It was like a light shone and the wind blew just on them, even inside. It took me a while to not stumble over my words like a bumbling idiot when talking directly to them.

John had a bit of a reputation for being difficult. In reality, they just wanted to be left alone to work together—Bo produced their movies; John directed—and create art. But some of his creative demands (he wanted all creative approvals) were hard to sell to a studio, even mine. I liked them both for their directness and honesty.

We agreed to meet next at an upcoming film market in Milan. They brought some advisors and reps. Their ultra-fame meant a mob anyplace we went, so I rented an entire small but charming restaurant for just our party. It was lovely. Plus, I wanted to impress them with my planning, care, and forethought.

That didn't last long.

I don't remember the details, but John quickly got into an argument with the waiter. Since it was only us that night, the restaurant had only one waiter. Voices escalated in Italian, so I don't really know who said what, but it resulted in the waiter ripping off his apron with overdramatic angry gestures out of an old Italian movie, throwing his apron on the ground, and now, in English, saying:

"I quit!"

He stamped on the apron, ran out the door, and was gone.

Without the waiter, there would be no dinner. Without the dinner, no chance for the sequel to *10*.

I ran after him. Outside, I couldn't see where he'd gone. A British kid was sitting on a bench in front of the restaurant. I asked if he'd seen where the guy had run. The kid said he took off and then veered off the main street down an alley. No way I could catch him.

The kid asked what happened.

I asked him if he spoke Italian. Turns out, he was a student, in Italy for the semester, studying Italian. He started to walk away.

No waiter, no dinner.

I yelled, "Wait—want to be a waiter tonight for John and Bo Derek? I'll pay you two hundred euro," I told him, all the cash I had.

He said, "Sure."

I brought him inside, introduced him to the table as our new waiter. Then, I marched him into the kitchen, and introduced him to the owner/chef as our new waiter.

The owner just shrugged and tossed the kid an apron.

The night turned out wonderful.

Here was a "just ask" situation where I had no time to decide or think about it. I didn't even ask the guy who owned the restaurant if I could do this. I had no idea who the kid was and didn't even learn anything more about him—what if he was a nutjob or serial killer?

Could I bet this seminal dinner on some kid I didn't know? What if he got in a worse fight with John, or did a terrible job?

In these situations, you simply must trust your instincts. No time for reflection, contemplation, or questioning. A touch of the madness to bet all this on a stranger I met two seconds earlier on the street in Milan? Absolutely. But I took the shot because it just felt right at the moment.

So sometimes you have to just ask from your gut, with no research, planning, or contingency.

One more story. Sometimes the asking goes well, but not how you originally thought. Be open to these twists and turns. They may surprise you in the most wonderful way.

NO SECRET, PRACTICE

Several years ago, I called Vietnamese Zen Master Thich Nhat Hanh, or Thay, meaning "teacher" in Vietnamese, as he was known.

Thay, a Buddhist monk, popularized the concept of mindfulness in the West. He was nominated for a Nobel Peace Prize by Martin Luther King, wrote over one hundred books, had millions of followers, and taught all over the world.

So what did I do? Called and asked this nonviolent Buddhist monk to be the inspiration for a character in *Mortal Kombat*.

After spending a few hours with him and some of the monks and nuns, I thought I had been on vacation for a week. I asked, "What's your secret?"

He said, "No secret, practice."

I said, "You mean, I could learn how to feel this way all the time?"

We became great friends. In addition to being a wise Zen master, Thay was also interesting and funny. I brought him to LA to speak to a bunch of Hollywood types—studio heads, directors—who said it changed their lives, and I began a practice of mindfulness I still do now.

Also, at his request, I made a documentary called *Mindfulness: Be Happy Now*, about his mindfulness teachings.

My call about *Mortal Kombat* resulted in a life-changing way of thinking and some great friendships.

DEAR POPE

By the way, I am presenting examples of when this strategy succeeded. It doesn't always. But so what? People still say no to me all the time. Recently, I wrote to the pope asking for something. You know, the *Pope* pope, in Italy. We received a lovely pass letter from the head of Vatican City, but so what?

No is just the beginning.

I have already sent a follow-up request.

I tell all these stories because this is incredibly important, relatively simple, and almost no one does it.

You be the ones who do. Ask.

I would like to challenge you to pick someone you want to know. It could be someone famous or someone at work or someone in your extended circle of contacts. Figure out why, of course—what you would ask them—and just reach out. When I first started doing this, in college, it was much harder—you had a telephone or a written-and-mailed letter. Now, with email, LinkedIn, texting, DMs, it is so much easier.

So why not give it a try? This week. What do you have to lose?

Ask Ask Ask.

Chapter Four

PLAY

Third way to cultivate a touch of the madness: play; have fun; play it all like a game; live in a state of play.

Studies show in a state of play you are more aware, more attuned to your environment, more open-minded. This leads to more innovation.

Avalanche-rescue dogs, who save lives, think they are playing. We can learn a lot from dogs.

It works, and plus, it's a fun way to live.

So how do you get your organization—and yourself—to be in a state of play or fun? Fun is a little more challenging these days, and I think it is wildly underrated. But there are four ways.

DIVERSITY—TRUE DIVERSITY

First—diversity, but true diversity.

This means diversity not just based on how someone looks, but where they are from, their culture, their beliefs, their family structures, how they grew up, their socioeconomic positions.

When you have this kind of diversity of culture, religion, race, age, gender, economics, geography, you become more open-minded. And it becomes fun and helpful.

Here is an example.

STAY CALM AND BOBBLE ON

We have been and continue to build with Microsoft and Nvidia a worldwide digital production pipeline for animated movies and live-action movies with a lot of visual effects. This is all done in Azure, a cloud application, using new Nvidia chips for digital rendering.

The goal is to make movies "from the world, for the world." But we found something unexpected: it also allows us to make movies WITH the world.

Here's what I mean. Our animated movie, *Bobbleheads*, the one with Cher, is about little creatures whose heads bobble. Bobbleheads are given out in the US at sporting events often.

It turns out dolls whose heads bobble, in other words, bobbleheads, were invented in India hundreds of years ago. Yup, hundreds of years. There is a lot of cultural history around them and different types of these dolls.

As we were trying to figure out how these characters' heads should bobble, and how often, and in what direction, we noticed a lot of the crew from India were bobbling their heads, without thinking about it, as they talked to us!

It was part of their culture. When we all realized this, they then became enormously helpful in a way we didn't predict. The movie became better; they were happy to culturally contribute; it became more playable to the whole world.

I think that's fun. It's so interesting and simply opens your mind when surrounded by so many different cultural outlooks.

These kinds of benefits from true diversity are fun and, if in a receptive state, like a state of play, lead to innovations.

Now, one thing. It can take a little time to learn how to interact with such diversity of cultures and thoughts.

The Special Forces have a saying, "Slow is smooth and smooth is fast." That is how you must look at true diversity. A little patience, especially at the beginning, goes a long, long way as you progress.

PAUL NEWMAN EYES

One animator on our worldwide network oversaw a character I wanted to look dashing, so I kept telling this animator to give the character "Paul Newman eyes." Paul Newman was a famous, good-looking movie star in the sixties, seventies, and early eighties, well known for his piercing blue eyes.

I would check everyone's work every week. This animator's was great. Did everything I asked. Except no Paul Newman eyes. I would tell him great job but remember: Paul Newman eyes on this one character. He would smile and nod.

———————————

After several weeks of this, I finally just said to him, "Your work is terrific, but you gotta tell me once and for all why you won't give this character Paul Newman eyes?"

He looked down, sheepishly, and asked, "Who's Paul Newman?"

I learned two things. First, culturally, where he was from, it was seen as disrespectful to question authority even if one did not understand. I over time learned how to interpret that cultural difference and slowly eliminate it so the artists could ask.

The second thing was: I learned Paul Newman was just too irrelevant of a reference. It meant nothing to these young animators, and thus would probably have no relevance to our audience. If our artists didn't even get the joke, how would the audience?

We changed the character. Diversity, true diversity, once again helped me make a better movie.

MAKE PLAY WORK FOR YOU

You can make play more than a phrase or saying; you can make it actually work for you. But you gotta go for it, embrace it.

PARTY IN MALIBU

There is a great producer/director in Greece we'll call Alex. No one got a better, richer look on the screen for little money than Alex.

He is also a great guy with a zest for life, kind of the movie business's version of Zorba the Greek.

One day at Vestron he pitched me a movie about a producer who rents a mansion on the beach in Malibu for the summer, stocks it with beautiful people, chefs, and DJs, and has a party all summer. I forget the plot, not that it mattered. A low-budget, great-looking Malibu summer beach party movie would work in those days.

I asked Alex how he would pull this off.

Easy, he said. We would give him money from the budget of a movie to rent a house on the beach in Malibu, stock it with beautiful people, chefs, and DJs.

He would also stock it with a camera crew and live there all summer.

"Let's do it, no?" he asked.

It sounded too good to be true—to film a great summer beach party movie, have a beach party all summer. The budget came in low as well. It sounded, well, too fun to be true.

But I did it.

Full disclosure—I spent a lot of time there that summer, too.

It was fun.

And the movie did great. Play worked for me.

THE FATE OF THE WORLD DEPENDS ON YOU . . .

Christopher Lambert is a famous French actor known for his iconic roles as the Highlander, the immortal swordsman of those eighties movies whose slogan was "There Can Be Only One"; as Tarzan, in *Greystoke: the Legend of Tarzan, Lord of the*

Apes; and as Rayden, god of thunder and defender of the realm of Earth in our first *Mortal Kombat* movie.

I didn't know Chris prior to *Mortal Kombat*. We were shooting in Thailand, in the mystical northern former capital Ayutthaya, when on a whim, Chris and I decided to take advantage of a weekend break in the schedule and explore Bangkok.

That weekend trip not only taught me the meaning of the song "One Night in Bangkok," it also made Chris and me instant friends to this day.

One of the things I learned about Chris that most people don't realize because of the tough-guy roles he plays is he is funny as hell.

Sometimes, he would just try to crack up everyone on set with a funny ad-libbed take or pantomime. I thought he was hysterical. I would encourage this.

He had a scene in the movie where Rayden says to the Earth Warriors, before they enter the parallel realm of Outworld to fight for Earth in a tournament called *Mortal Kombat*, "The fate of the world depends on you."

We tried the scene a few times, and it just came off as too on-the-nose corny. We weren't sure what to do because it was a pivotal moment in the movie.

Without being asked, Chris ad-libbed a take where he said, "The fate of the earth depends on you"—then he looked at them all with disbelief, cracked up laughing, as if to say, there is no way you nerds can pull this off, and said, "Sorry." And went back into character.

Everyone laughed. And then kept laughing.

And then we decided to use it in the movie. It not only plays great but helped define the character of Rayden in many more *Mortal Kombat* productions as a fun, wiseass god of thunder.

Chris's and my state of play got us one of the best lines in a hit movie and helped make one of the greatest characters of the franchise come to life.

Had we not experienced that wild weekend in Bangkok together, would I have been so open, and would Chris have felt so creatively free? I'm not saying always take the opportunity for a wild weekend— well, I guess I sort of am—but also, live in a state of play to maximize innovation.

A NIGHT AT THE PLAYBOY MANSION

In addition to movies, we also make theme park rides. A few years ago, we were negotiating a deal to create a high-end, classy, location-based entertainment experience called "A Night at the Playboy Mansion." It was going to premiere in London and Shanghai.

I almost had the deal closed with Playboy but not quite.

Before Playboy sold the mansion, every Halloween, they would throw the world's best party: tons of interesting, fun people; lavish food and great cookies; six acres of lush gardens in Beverly Hills with its own actual zoo; an amazing haunted house and everyone decked out in elaborate costumes.

The guy slated to direct our location-based experience dared me to go dressed as a Playmate.

Everyone told me it was a bad idea. My brother said it was the worst he had ever heard. Even my old friend, who owns an erotic boutique, told me point-blank not to do it.

So of course, I did it.

I learned two things.

I really went all out: fishnet stockings, fake boobs, the Playmate costume that looks kind of like a one-piece bathing suit, long wig, makeup, and everything. It took so long to get dressed.

Then, I went to a salon to have my makeup done. I told them to just make it look like I tried, but don't go crazy or anything. It still took an hour.

I've always been thin. But when I finally looked at myself in the mirror, dressed as a Playmate in tight clothes and fishnet stockings, wig, and makeup, a kind of verbal bolt of lightning struck me, and without even realizing it, I said something out loud to myself I never have:

"Do my thighs look fat in these stockings?"

Then, shocked at what I had somehow just blurted out, I looked around. Where did that come from? I'd never even thought that, let alone said it.

I think there should be a law that every guy, once in his life, has to dress up like a woman, just to understand what most women go through simply to get out the door.

I thought I knew. I approve costumes for women in my movies. I like fashion photography.

Turns out I had no idea.

It takes me maybe sixty seconds to get ready—sneakers, jeans, polo shirt, baseball cap, done.

When I dressed and did makeup for the Halloween party, I was exhausted before I even left for the event. It took hours. I felt like I'd been getting ready for a play. I have not since then ever said to a woman who was getting ready: "Hurry up."

Just to understand, please try it.

But the real first thing I learned of course was this lesson. You must always be open that when you apply a touch of the madness to your life or a situation, you might just learn something unexpected. I did. Please be open to that.

OK, shock of my thighs wearing off, I went to the party.

Now, I had no idea how this would be received by the execs at Playboy. Remember, while this was fun and I was certainly trying to make play work for me, I was attending for work, to close a deal. I really had no experience showing up to a work event dressed as a Playmate.

But the current will pull you towards the middle if you don't swim against it, and I am not a fan of the middle, so off I went.

I was a hit!

Everyone seemed to find my costume fascinating. I met tons of people and had a blast.

And the Playboy execs and the director were so impressed, not with how I looked as a woman, trust me, but that I committed, and went for it, and put so much thought and time and effort into this (Playmate) costume for their party, we closed the deal.

Play worked for me again. Please try it. You can have fun, close your deal, and maybe even learn something unexpected. Plus you might look good in fishnet stockings.

THE GREAT VEGETABLE ATTACK AT CANNES

Here is another example.

We're at the Cannes Film Festival in the South of France in May, raising money for *True Lies*.

One night, we all go to a black-tie dinner at the Hotel Du Cap. I think this hotel is the epitome of casual elegance in the world. F. Scott Fitzgerald's characters partied there in some of his novels. It's still the same. Set on dramatic cliffs and lush gardens on the Mediterranean in Antibes, it's been for years the ultra-classy epicenter of the Cannes Film Festival.

I'm at a table, as I recall, with people like Jim Cameron and Arnold Schwarzenegger. Most everyone at the dinner is gorgeous and famous. It is a fundraiser for something really important, which unfortunately I forget.

While trying to look serious and pay attention to the presentation, when I really want to look around and gawk at the audience, I feel something whiz past me. It isn't a bug. I shrug it off.

A minute later, something hits me. It's a pea. Like the kind on our plates, that you eat.

Must be some fluke.

Another few minutes go by, and now more peas. An onslaught. As if we are being shelled in World

War I but with peas. And other vegetables. Now other people at our table notice, too.

I look around. A few tables back, I see Jamie Lee Curtis, giggling. I had made a movie with Jamie a few years earlier, called *Blue Steel*, that Kathryn Bigelow directed. But it wasn't like we were close pals.

Could Jamie be the culprit?

No way.

But then, more peas, more food comes sailing over. In my recollection, she was laughing hysterically.

Jim turns to me and suggests we think about her for the lead female role in *True Lies*. That was a great idea!

And Jamie did wind up playing the lead in *True Lies*. She was awesome. In fact, over the years, more people tell me her scene where she turned out goofy when she tried to be sexy for her superspy husband, Arnold, who was drugged and didn't know it was her, was their favorite in the movie. With all the effects and Harrier jets, her performance stood out. That's a great actress.

Now, I cannot prove Jamie threw the peas and was the evil perpetrator of a would-be food fight at a charity event at the nicest hotel on the French Riviera. I mean, I think she was but no proof. An agent a few days later told me he ran into her earlier the day of the dinner and mentioned we had not yet cast the female lead in *True Lies*. And whether she was or wasn't the pea thrower, Jim might have thought of her anyway and cast her, pea cannons or not, or might have already thought of it.

But I hope she did it on purpose. I hope that was the catalyst that nailed her the role. Because what a great example of being in a state of play, making play work for you, and embracing a touch of the madness to land a lead role in a hit movie in which she excelled.

I hope so.

PLAY IT LIKE A GAME

If you can play your innovation and creativity at work like a game, you will do better.

Now, we all think of playing like it's a game as not taking it seriously. I doubt champion athletes would agree. A heavyweight boxer or NFL quarterback or tennis player at Wimbledon takes their "game" seriously. But it doesn't mean they don't play it like one.

If you can see professional challenges that way, you will approach them with a more open mind, like when you were a kid and came up with more creative, out-of-the-box solutions.

That's innovation.

Play it like a game. Here is an example.

THE NEVER-ENDING CAR RIDE

When I was putting together the financing for *True Lies*, I was introduced by our then agents at ICM to a great guy in Germany named Jürgen Wohlrabe. As soon as we met, at a film festival in Italy, we started negotiating, then screaming at each other, then laughing.

He reminded me of my Eastern European grandparents, whose natural tone of voice was yelling. Jürgen was a fascinating guy, once, I think, head of the Berlin senate, and now owner and CEO of his own successful independent film distribution company.

After a few months of more meetings across Europe much like the first—all yelling and laughing, like we were playing a game, which we were—finally, we made a deal. He was to license the German rights for the movie.

The way this kind of financing works is the producer slices up the distribution rights to the film like a pie, charging everyone a percentage for their slice (distribution rights in their territory). The whole equals 100 percent. The producer takes all these contracts to a bank, borrows the money based on them, then delivers the movie when done to all the distributors, who then pay.

There is a little—well, not so little—thing called "withholding tax" in some countries. This is a local tax that is usually 10 percent of the license fee. The distributors always pay their own withholding tax, meaning it really costs them 10 percent more than they pay us.

True Lies was an expensive movie. The withholding tax for Germany alone was in the seven figures, as I recall.

When we gathered all the paperwork from all the distributors to show the bank, we noticed Jürgen slipped into his contract a clause that he wouldn't pay the withholding tax.

So just like the closing of the sale of a house, if something is missing—here, seven figures of money—the whole deal won't close.

Everyone became furious. I smiled to myself, thinking it was just good ol' Jürgen taking a shot. It was just a game. One point for him. But what to do?

Coincidentally, we found out he was coming to LA in a few days. There were no cell phones then, so we called all the limo companies in town that picked people up at the airport. We found his, pretended to be his office, so we got the flight info, and cancelled the limo.

When Jürgen came out of customs at LAX, tired from his flight from Germany, wanting nothing more than to go to his hotel and eat and sleep, instead he saw me, wearing a chauffeur's cap, with one of those little signs with his name on it.

He stopped and let out an exasperated sigh—one point for me. He then smiled and said his trademark, "I am HERE!"

I said, "Where to, sir?" He told me his hotel.

When we settled in my car, I started driving and said, "You realize of course I am not letting you out of this car until you sign the right contract, where you pay the withholding tax."

We drove around LA for three hours, screaming at each other.

Finally, he laughed and signed. I knew he was going to. He was just taking a shot. Had it worked, he would have saved over a million dollars. This way, he just lost three hours.

Then we went to dinner.

"You pay," he said.

LIVE IN A STATE OF PLAY

If you want to be in good shape, you exercise all the time, not just the day before you go to the doctor. If you want to be anxiety free, you mediate all the time, not just when you worry.

Similarly, if you want to be the most innovative you can and add a touch of the madness to your life, I suggest you try to live in a state of play all the time. My dog does, and it works for him. He views everything as a game and he is the happiest creature I know.

But first, here is an example when I didn't.

"I'M GREAT!"

At Vestron, I inherited an art film division that had made some movies, sort of. I mean, they were shot, but either not very good technically, or lacking things like the rights for the music that was in them, and so forth. My job was to fix them.

One had a performance by the lead actress that just wasn't good enough. I told the executive once responsible for the movies, who now reported to me, we would have to dub her performance with another actress's voice. This means another actress kind of secretly records the voice performance of the main actress pictured on film.

Now, the original actress was really a nice person, and pretty famous at the time. It probably wasn't even her fault—so many factors go into this: the director, the other actors, the script—but it didn't matter, the movie comes first. The audience (remember, we work for them) just wants to be entertained; the behind-the-scenes problems are not theirs.

In those days, we threw a lot of big movie premieres. These fancy screenings with red carpets and lavish parties were designed for one thing—to get press. No Instagram or Facebook in those days—press meant a big article in a huge publication, like the *New York Times*, or a piece on the network evening news or CNN.

At this premiere, I was to sit next to the lead actress during the screening. This was nothing at all personal—I was the head of the studio; she was the glamorous star—the publicists arranged this for the press.

A few minutes before the screening started, I asked the executive once in charge how the actress had taken the news her performance had been dubbed when he told her.

"Oh, I didn't tell her," he said. "I thought you would."

Mind you, there was press everywhere, and we had to look happy and great.

What could I do?

Now, I gotta admit, I did not take this in a state of play. The screening was like four minutes from starting. We were mobbed by press and other celebrity guests (all invited to generate, yes, more press). I couldn't tell her then.

I kept imagining a disaster when she realized in the middle of the screening what we did, freaked out, and screamed, or yelled, or cried. All pretty human reactions to finding out your voice is not yours during the premiere of your movie.

It was one of the longest screenings I've ever sat through—well, it seemed that way to me—as I pictured the downfall of my career in the headlines.

The movie ended. The moment of my imagined doom arrived.

The lights came up. During the applause, she turned to me. I cringed, bracing for the fallout.

Eyes wide, surprise on her face, she said, "Wow! I had no idea I was that good! I love it! Thank you thank you thank you."

She had no idea we dubbed her. Unless she is reading this, she still doesn't.

The point is: My worrying and cringing did nothing but spoil a few hours for me. I learned that you never know how these things will turn out. Had she noticed, in a state of play, I could have said, "No one will know and you come off great" or "Let's talk about the sequel." I never even thought of that in my disaster planning.

But I didn't have to. Why she didn't notice, I will never know. Who cares? Movie first, and I learned to take these things in a state of play!

Here's one that did work.

THE AMAN HAS A YACHT, YOU SAY?

Recently a friend who runs her own successful consulting company called to ask why she feels guilty about taking an hour off during the day to do something fun, like knit. She makes her own hours; it doesn't affect anything—she just works an hour later on days like that—but she still doesn't feel "right" doing it.

Most people tend to equate fun and play with goofing off, not doing the right job.

I equate it with a touch of the madness, with being creative and innovative and open.

Mortal Kombat was the first movie of a new company I started, and I did everything possible to make sure it succeeded. I worked around the clock. I took it incredibly seriously. But that does not mean I gave up a chance to play when it worked for me.

We found ourselves shooting in the Andaman Sea in Southern Thailand off the coast of Krabi. This is one of the most beautiful places in the world. Majestic limestone outcroppings dotted with vegetation stand spread out in the emerald-green water of the bay.

It makes you feel like you are in another world, which is exactly why we picked the location.

We needed some "B roll" of the water and limestone rock formations and the island. "B roll" means establishing shots with no actors. Usually, a small splinter crew shoots it.

In this case, we couldn't find a boat that would work. The local fishermen helped us a lot, but their boats were too small and unsteady for the cameras.

Near Krabi is Phuket, a resort town and home of the Amanpuri, the first in a chain of Zen, luxury hotels.

Turns out the Amanpuri has a yacht you can rent.

Well, I of course decided this B roll was important and I must supervise it myself.

Did I spend three days cruising the Andaman Sea with a camera crew on the Aman yacht? Think you have figured out the answer.

Now, this was all in the budget, totally legit, and we succeeded in capturing great shots.

Boats and movies are two of my favorite things in the world. Why should I feel guilty or funny about combining them to help my movie, which it did?

Well, I didn't. I felt great. I think it's crazy to feel otherwise. But everyone I tell kind of laughs and nods knowingly, like I pulled a fast one. What I did was capture stunning location shots of amazing islands, using the best boat for the job in the area.

And yes, had a blast. I don't think the crew would have worked that hard if they weren't having as much fun.

Next time you have an opportunity to play while doing your job, take it. You will feel better in general and probably see more innovative results in your work.

And finally, you must learn to live in a state of play even when the situation is somewhat . . . extreme.

SNAKES AND WIZARDS

When I became head of production at Vestron, the company had already committed to one movie: a fantasy, *Game of Thrones*–type of film, but for like one-millionth the budget.

The producer was one of my favorite scoundrels —I use that word affectionately—from the time; Roger, we'll call him.

Roger reminded me of a character from a Charles Dickens novel. Short, always in a disheveled suit, British, and charming, he carried a portable typewriter, writing scripts on endless plane rides to make deals, surviving, it seemed, on chocolate bars and Scotch.

But he made lots of movies.

Our movie was to be shot in Rome. Roger was already there, prepping it.

My boss told my staff and me he wanted "violence, sword fighting, sex, wild parties—you name it—everything, even snakes and wizards!" he said with a chuckle. We were all laughing and having fun, and we got the idea.

For some reason, we, the studio staff in LA, latched on to the phrase "snakes and wizards" in an affectionate, long-ago way. It became our battle cry to each other.

And when we spoke to Roger in Rome before I got there, we would always end our phone calls with, "And remember, snakes and wizards!"

We forgot Roger was not in on the joke. More on that in a second.

Now, weeks later, I am in Rome. Great food, scenery, nice crew.

And Roger and the crew keep telling me they have a surprise for me. They are so excited, it seems, counting down the days.

Finally, the big day of my surprise comes. They take me out back, where I could see dirt roads stretch for miles into the fields. The sun is setting.

But nothing.

Then I see a little cloud of dust in the distance. It grows. A truck approaching.

As it gets closer, I can see it appears to be a circus truck.

The entire cast and crew assemble in a semicircle behind me, Roger next to me. Beaming.

The truck stops, backs up.

Music starts playing. I have no idea where they found a band.

The doors burst open and out charges female snake charmers with huge Burmese pythons and boa constrictors around their necks, surrounded by people wonderfully costumed as wizards.

Everyone applauds. They are so proud of themselves. They got us our snakes and wizards!

Except there was just one thing. There were no snakes and wizards in the movie. It was a joke, an exaggeration. We just forgot to tell Roger.

So what to do? I could have been mad at all the time and money they spent. I could have freaked out.

But I also felt I couldn't tell him at that point we had been kidding—they obviously went to great lengths and were so proud. Plus, it is kind of hard to say no to a twelve-foot Burmese python staring you in the face.

And it was kind of a blast. Like a party in medieval times. I did the only thing I could.

I put all the snakes and wizards in the movie. Somehow, they fit. And it turned out great.

Well, the movie is kind of terrible. But it did make a ton of money and the snakes were terrific.

And what fun.

———

So here I am telling you about snakes in Rome and bobbleheads in India and parties in Malibu. Here is my question.

What fun thing have you always kind of wished for, dreamed of, or fantasized about doing at work that you haven't done?

Maybe you wanted to take your staff bowling. Or fossil hunting. Or on a hot-air balloon ride. Or to the museum for a drawing class.

OK, now, your challenge is: Go do it. Tomorrow.

Chapter Five

A TOUCH—NOT A TON— OF THE MADNESS

CAN YOU GO TOO FAR?

Where is the line between a touch of the madness and, say, a ton of the madness?

Obviously, I am not recommending you go crazy nuts and embrace insanity. But how do you know when it's too much?

Only you can tell what is right for you.

Be yourself first and foremost. You can't fake a touch of the madness and have it help your creativity and innovation, so I would not bother trying. All you will wind up with is meaningless virtue signaling.

The point here is to embrace your true creative self, with no internal barriers or limiting thoughts, and wind up with great innovation.

Here are some, let's call them "case studies," all with the question: A touch or a ton of the madness?

IF YOU THOUGHT LANDING WAS BAD, TAKEOFF IS WORSE

After 9/11, I was on a committee of Hollywood types gathered to brainstorm disaster scenarios and scare tactics we would have terrorists use in a movie. The Pentagon sponsored this as a way of thinking outside the box and perhaps anticipating next moves based on our imagined scenarios.

We gathered under such unfortunate circumstances, of course, but it was fascinating. I met a lot of people from the military, some still friends, and had the idea to develop a movie based on some of what I'd learned.

Sitting in my office soon after, with my creative team working on the script, we realized if we had some real exposure to these guys in the field, it would help us (OK, and be fun).

But what training mission could we observe that would be most productive?

"Weapons training," someone said.

"Watching Navy SEAL training down in San Diego," another yelled out.

Then I said, "You know what would be so cool—to land on a US aircraft carrier at sea! Let's do that."

I didn't think much more about it, but one of my staff really latched on to the idea and arranged for it.

Cut to a few weeks later, and a small group of us were standing on the tarmac at a Navy air base in Southern California. We wore crash helmets, fire-retardant crash gear, life preservers, and helmets with walkie-talkies in them.

The commanding officer explained we would be flying via a small troop transport Navy jet. There would be no windows for security reasons; we could not know the location of the carrier we were going to, only that it was in the Pacific Ocean. Communication was via headset only. There would be life rafts inflated in the small cabin. Should we ditch—crash into the water—we should get in one.

It all kind of scared me. I hadn't really thought about it that deeply, more suggested it on a whim. I wondered, *Have I gone too far into the madness this time?*

I pretended to go to the bathroom but really called my then girlfriend to ask if I should bail. Given my girlfriend at the time was an Olympic gold medalist in Tae Kwon Do, a top Hollywood stuntwoman, and a master equestrian, in hindsight I now realize her answer would be obvious: "Oh, go for it!"

So I did. Stomach doing butterflies and all.

What the CO didn't tell us is when a jet lands on an aircraft carrier, it doesn't land like your lovely

British Air flight gently descending and then gliding down into London as if on a feather while they offer you a final drink.

In case it is followed or tracked on enemy radar, the jet does not slowly descend at all.

It finds the aircraft carrier when the jet is at full altitude, gets close, then heads almost straight down. (You will note this is not a technical description.)

This is called a "carrier break." I kept hearing over the headphones in my crash helmet: "Prepare for carrier break (static)"; "Thirty seconds to carrier break"; "Carrier break commenced."

But I did not know this. As we were plummeting what seemed like straight down, with crash gear, no windows, lifeboats around us, I again thought, *Did I go too far?*

I had a moment of calm and figured if we crashed into the Pacific, at least I would go out grabbing a touch of the madness.

Fortunately, that did not happen.

At the last second, the jet leveled out and executed a controlled crash into the carrier at about 125 miles an hour. The jet was caught by a trip wire, which stops it. Sometimes, I learned later, the trip wire misses, and the pilot has something like two seconds to take off again or it's into the drink.

We emerged, shaken and stirred, into the sunlight on the carrier flight deck, into a world that at first looked like chaos, but soon revealed itself as a marvel of technology and teamwork and talent. The pilot, by the way, still had his tie fully tied, all hairs in place, as if posing for a *GQ* ad, not a bead of sweat, while we looked like wrecks.

They can launch a jet something like every twenty seconds, so they can deploy a team into the air in an hour. One US carrier has more firepower than most countries. The amazement started to chase away my butterflies, plus the gratitude of not being in a raft in the ocean, of course.

Just then, Klaxon alarms went off.

Loudspeaker: "Unidentified aircraft approaching from west. Two hundred and fifty miles out. Go."

Everyone started to move in synchronized, rehearsed, rushed order. We were gently but firmly pushed against a wall just off the flight deck.

"Don't move a muscle," we were ordered.

Jets zoomed off the floating tarmac.

This was only a few years after the USS *Cole*, a US aircraft carrier, was bombed in the Persian Gulf, and only about a year after 9/11.

Loudspeaker: "Aircraft not responding to comm [communications]. Assume hostile. This is not a drill. Repeat: this is not a drill."

Hundreds of military personnel moving even faster. More jets in the air.

"One hundred miles out. Engage [which means 'attack']."

"This is not a drill."

OK, once again, I was thinking, *Have I gone too far?*

Turns out it was a drill.

Whew!

We then had lunch with the admiral in his dining room, great view of the flight deck. Lots of pilots there. All of us visitors were relieved we landed OK, relieved it was a drill, and, overall, just incredibly impressed.

After the lovely lunch and really interesting briefing on what we would see the rest of the day, the admiral asked if there were any questions.

I raised my hand.

"Yes, sir?" he said with bold confidence.

"Can we go waterskiing after lunch?" I asked.

OK, clearly, I was kidding. But here I think I went too far. I thought it was hysterical. He did not seem to think so. He never said anything negative but didn't laugh. More on this later.

We spent a fascinating afternoon seeing the ship and all the functions. But just one thing kind of bothered me. All the pilots and brass asked me how I felt about landing on a carrier at sea. I would always laugh and tell them it was scary but amazing.

They all said, "Oh, if you think landing was hard, wait until you take off. It's way worse."

This happened so many times the ol' butterflies were coming back. By around five o'clock, I was plotting how to find a helicopter to airlift me off the boat the next day.

Anyway, finally, we were taken to our bunks. The inside of the ship looked kind of like an Escher print, or a Terry Gilliam movie. There were gray hallways and stairs in every direction. It was hard to get bearings or figure out where exactly I was.

We were, I think, eleven stories down, right smack in the middle of the ship. It was ever so slightly moving from the ocean, so it made me a skootch light-headed.

Our military-like bunk beds were fine but nondescript. They all looked the same, in every direction, and up and down.

The guide, a private, said to us, "Now, what is important, most important, is you DO NOT leave your bunk at night. Under any circumstances. We will come get you at 0:700. Got it?"

Everyone, trying to be military, said, "Yes, sir!"

The private turned around as he was leaving. "Remember, do not leave your bunks."

So, later that night, I of course left my bunk.

I started climbing up the flights of stairs. I just had to see what it all looked like at night.

Was this going too far? I didn't think so, at the time. I doubted they would throw me overboard (although after my waterskiing comment, not so sure). And how many times would I get this opportunity?

I found my way somehow to the observation deck, way above everything. And they were doing night ops—turning the boat into the wind (better for takeoffs) and taking off and landing jets, at night, on a boat in the middle of the rough, wavy ocean, one a minute. Inspiring.

And I got to watch it for quite a while, at night on a US aircraft carrier at sea. Just me. Alone.

Or so I thought.

After a while, I noticed I was not alone. There was a soldier I literally almost bumped into. The observation deck was big, but I was still surprised we had not noticed each other before. *That's it,* I thought, *I'm busted.* I tried to be friendly and struck up a conversation first.

He didn't look like the polished officers and pilots I had been meeting. Looked more like a regular soldier. He stood before an old rotary-dial telephone, just staring out to sea.

I explained I was one of the visiting movie people. I was trying to set myself up for a "I had no idea I wasn't supposed to be here," but he never asked.

I asked what he did.

"Well, sir, I look that way." He pointed out to sea in the direction he was looking.

"And then what?"

"Well, if I see something, I pick up this phone [the old rotary one] and I dial a number and tell them what I see."

It occurred to me that because I was not out to sea, e.g., "that way," I was not part of his job, so it was like I never even registered.

I asked if he liked his work. He told me he loved it; he knew everywhere he was supposed to be and everything he was supposed to do, from his duty roster to the ice cream socials, for the next six months.

I then realized that while an aircraft carrier has five thousand people on it, they really try to introduce the movie types to only the flashier ones, like the pilots and admirals. But less-glamorous guys like this were equally important; the ship could not function without them.

So this part was worth it for that lesson. Being open to learning the unexpected from a touch of the madness, like at the Playboy Mansion, I did learn.

Now, only two more obstacles. I had to find my way through the maze back to my bunk. And I had to figure out how to get off the ship in some way that wasn't more harrowing than the landing!

I did find my way back to the bunk, and never got caught, although I am not sure exactly how that happened.

Unfortunately, all efforts for helicopters, row boats, and jet skis home of course failed. More and more pilots told me at breakfast the next morning how bad takeoff would be.

They then added a part and told me how it works.

Once again, we would wear crash suits and helmets and go back into a windowless cabin with an inflated life raft. Then, our jet would get catapulted—literally—off the deck. It goes from zero to 120 miles per hour in two seconds. When the jet clears the carrier, it falls—loses altitude—before the thrust kicks in. So we would be careening towards the ocean at 120 mph.

They told me in every scary way imaginable.

Again, the thought, *Too far?*

Turns out, taking off is not worse, it's easier. No walk in the park, mind you—it's like getting punched in the stomach for a few seconds, and then falling, which is scary but quick before the thrust kicks in.

So they were screwing with me. I think they did it to get back at me for the waterskiing joke. Well played.

At the end of the day, was the whole thing worth it, or too far? We heard the next week—but not confirmed—a pilot was killed during a mishap at takeoff. There were real risks.

It was worth it, and I don't think too far. Here is why.

First, I saw amazing things, met incredible people —from the pilots to the "I look that way" soldier.

And *Top Gun*, if anything, underplays it. I don't care who you are or what your politics are, but if you experience what I did and don't feel a sense of pride and awe, you are made of stone. I never really understood this before.

These are all great things to put in a movie, and just to learn. Mission accomplished.

Second, my only reason for not doing it would have been fear. I wanted to go; I was just scared a few times. But I did it anyway and wound up glad I did.

Most people will do more to avoid what they fear than to go after what they want. Try not to be one of them.

If you don't want to do something, if it seems so crazy it is just unappealing, don't do it. But if you want to do it, and fear is your only obstacle, do the opposite of what the fear is telling you and grab a touch of the madness.

But don't screw around with any admirals you might meet.

THE ALIENS WILL EAT MY CHILDREN

One of the movies we were thinking about making in the Vestron days was based on a hit book about the alien abduction of the author. No kidding—he claimed furry little space creatures (well, as I remember it they were furry) snatched him up, experimented, gave him orders—the whole deal.

This movie was still in development, meaning we had commissioned the author of the book to write a script for a film based on the book but had not yet green-lit the movie. Standard procedure in Hollywood.

Now, whether or not I believed this guy was buzzing around the universe with Gorthop the Alien wasn't the point. There is a section of the audience that eats this stuff up, true or not.

But it still had to be a good movie, which usually starts with a good script, and his wasn't, in my opinion. And he would not take the constructive notes on how to fix the script from any of my staff.

He asked to meet with me alone. So I went to see him, and it was just the two of us.

After I explained the issues we had with the script, and how a movie works (different from a book because we will see everything but can't hear what the main character is thinking), he told me with seemingly great sincerity he was so relieved I came to see him.

There was something he couldn't tell my staff, but he could confide in me (by the way, I hardly knew this guy).

"What is it?" I asked.

"Well." He surreptitiously looked left, then right. Then leaned forward and lowered his voice.

"Well, *they*—" This time, he pointed up to the sky. "*They*—" He pointed again and made it clear he was talking about the aliens. "*They* want this story to be told. And *they* want it told the way I wrote it in the script."

"Do *they* want a hit movie?" I asked.

"Well, *they*"—more pointing—"*they* said if I don't tell it their way, *they* will abduct my children." He seemed teary.

I said, "Let me get this straight. You are telling me if we don't do the script your way, the space aliens will steal your children and take them from you and do terrible things to them, like eat them or something?"

He told me yes, that is exactly what will happen.

I waited a minute, then reached out to shake his hand. He thought I was going to agree.

"Congratulations," I said. "That is the wildest reason for a writer ignoring the studio's notes I ever heard. You should win a prize! 'Do what I want, or the aliens will eat my kids!' It's almost brilliant."

Now, it *was* almost brilliant. It was so far out there it really should get a prize. But was it going too far?

I think if he really believed it, he deserved to be with a studio that believed in him.

If he didn't believe it himself, which was my gut opinion, he was being fake, and that would bleed into any movie he made, in my opinion.

I do think this was going too far, as we nor anyone else ever made the movie.

No news on how the kids are doing.

REALLY STRANGE DAYS

We were developing a movie called *Strange Days*. Kathryn Bigelow (*The Hurt Locker*) was going to direct. It's about a future technology that allowed someone to "play back" the experiences of another. So you could look, see, feel, hear, and smell what it was like to be a bank robber or a downhill skier or a rock star.

We needed for research to learn more about underground raves in LA. This was a long time ago, when raves really were secret, not easily found, hard to get into, clandestine, and wild.

Some of the team from the film and I found a kind of rave guide. I don't really remember how we found him, but the plan was for this kid to take us in a van all around downtown LA one night where he had prearranged our entry into a bunch of raves.

Exciting and simple, right? What could go wrong?

At one of the stops, the guide took us through a labyrinth of back alleys to a kind of holding area of a partially wrecked building with walls but no roof, as we waited to get in. A, let's call them, colorful collection of characters surrounded us. I tried to look cool, of course.

But then, the guy two in front of us pulled a gun on the guy in front of us. Like a real gun in real life in a back alley at a secret rave in downtown LA at 3 AM.

Did we go too far?

Well, you can't exactly say in a situation like that, "Excuse me, we're just the movie people, we're not really part of this, so we're just going to scoot off before the stray bullets start flying."

Actually, we were all calm, and our guide and someone else defused the situation (not even sure what he said to the guy with the gun). Everything sort of went back to normal, the line re-formed.

And we stayed. Then went in. We didn't even leave.

Is this too far?

Well, we didn't think so then, and I don't now. Yes, it had an element of danger to it, but we were looking to learn the real feel of these raves in those days, and that was the risk. I think it provided great research for the movie, which was our prime directive.

Sometimes, now, if I am in a crowded line for a concert, I think, well, at least no one's got a gun.

GORO THE SHOKAN MEETS PACO THE PANTHER

For our first *Mortal Kombat* movie, we built an animatronic creature named Goro. Eight feet high, fierce as can be, Goro sported four deadly arms. *Mortal Kombat* fans loved the deadly Goro.

He was one of the most advanced animatronic creatures ever built, and one of the last, as everything moved to digital after that. It took a team of operators to move Goro, including one guy inside the massive suit. Wires ran from him everywhere, that, of course, you could not see on-screen.

Goro turned out great, thanks to our terrific creature effects team.

But I thought: *You know what would make him even cooler? If he had a pet panther.*

In those days, if you wanted a panther on a movie, you found a trainer with a panther and hired them both. Today, no way you would expose a crew to that risk or an animal to that stress—it is all digital.

Not too far from LA, in the middle of the desert, sat a ranch that trained animals to be in movies. I love animals and was friendly with the owner/trainer, so I used to go up there all the time, using any excuse I could muster. It was a ramshackle cluster of an old house, huts, cages, containers.

I would play with tigers and lions and baboons on these trips.

And in the front yard, tied up like the family dog, a spotted black panther named Paco hung out. I used to play with Paco, too.

Now, I was going to give Paco his moment in the spotlight.

Or so I thought.

Paco came on set the first day, and Goro turned, raised his arms, and shouted his war cry.

Paco freaked out. Went nuts. Snarled. Hissed. Tried to break his chains and attack, or then run. We tried everything—secured with more chains, moved Goro far away, had Goro mellow out, fed Paco.

Nothing worked. Paco the panther would not tolerate Goro, Prince of the Shokan and General of the Armies of Outworld.

Even though we could keep the crew safe, we just felt so bad for Paco we quickly nixed his role.

Now, is this going too far with a touch of the madness? I already had Goro, one of the most advanced animatronic creatures ever built at the time. I could easily have been satisfied with just Goro, who turned in a terrific performance on his own.

This is a tough call. I probably should have realized what would happen. Maybe it is a testament to how well Goro was built that Paco thought him real?

And as I said, today, we would never do it, but that was not the case then.

What do you think: Paco the Panther meets Goro the Shokan—a touch or a ton of the madness?

Bottom line, right or wrong, I always would have been kicking myself, wondering what if, had I not tried. And while Goro was great, Goro with a panther really would have been better. And no one was hurt. Paco's ego might have been bruised when we cut his role, though.

The worst part is I never saw Paco again. I miss that guy.

"EH, POLITICIANS!"

Several years ago, when tensions were especially high in the Middle East, I sat in a London hotel room watching a CNN report on a terrorist attack in Israel, trying to make one of the hardest decisions of my life.

Do I take my film crew in London, shooting a sequel to *Mortal Kombat*, on to Israel and then Jordan for location shooting, as had been planned?

As the film's producer and one of the writers, and the guy who picked the location, I felt responsible for the one hundred American and British members of my crew, and for the additional crew members we were going to pick up in Israel and Jordan.

At that time, no one, as far as we knew, had ever shot in Jordan with a mixed Israeli/Jordanian crew. The security experts warned me that terrorists look for "press-worthy targets"; a Hollywood film certainly fits that description.

What if someone were hurt? Or killed. I'm the first to admit this was just a movie. Was it worth the risk?

Was this too much of the madness, to the point of actual danger?

But then I thought, what if we didn't go? The movie presented a great opportunity for people from different cultures to show they could work together. I like to think movies can bring different cultures together. Here would be proof. What if I let fear and uncertainty change my way—our way—of life?

We went.

Our first day in Jordan took us to the mystical, awe-inspiring, two-thousand-year-old city of Petra. It's called "The Rose Red City Half as Old as Time." There is no place like it in the world—over a mile of majestic, Nabatean temples built into a towering red-rock river valley in the Jordanian desert, near where Moses was born.

Petra was "lost" to the West from about the year 200 to the late 1800s, when a British explorer, dressed as a native, came across it. Punishment for visiting as an outsider: death.

The Israelis, up until the nineties, when the Jordanian/Israeli border was opened, couldn't go. There were rumors that Israeli daredevils every now and then would try to sneak in and see the fabled city, with dire consequences if caught.

Information about it was so scarce, when scouting locations a few months prior, we were not even sure what was there.

It is so magical, you really think, for the first day or two, it can't be real.

On our first day, after getting settled, about forty of us explored a little shop with a dirt floor. Eti, our Israeli co-producer, talked to the shopkeeper in varied tongues as our mixed crew of Arabs, British, and Americans milled about, laughing.

Then the shopkeeper asked Eti where she was from.

"Tel Aviv," she said.

Dead silence. The shopkeeper's face dropped. No one spoke. He backed away from her. Arabs and Westerners backed away from each other.

"Where are you from?" Eti asked.

"Baghdad," he replied. "And I had to leave my family to come here to find a living when your people destroyed my city."

Now she backed away.

Everyone stiffened, stared with trepidation at the person they were just laughing with.

Guys clenched their fists, as Arabs and Western-ers squared off.

Eti and the shopkeeper remained staring at each other for what seemed a long time.

Then one—I don't remember who—waved their hand dismissively and said, "Eh, politicians, what do they know!?"

Eti and the shopkeeper laughed and hugged. Tea appeared. Everyone relaxed, drank, and laughed again.

And it was like that for the rest of the shoot. Everyone worked together. Everyone had fun. I saw tough Israelis cry because they had never before seen their country from the east; and they could not believe they could not only see the fabled Rose Red City but also be welcomed there.

Jordanians made friends with Israelis and asked us about life in America. Some asked if they could come back with us to see it. My on-location Jorda-nian assistant invited me to his house for dinner.

I took a big risk, but I would take it again. I think now it would have been crazy not to.

And we leaned in to it. We told everyone. CNN came to do a story on us. I wrote about it for *USA Today*.

Chapter Six

EMBRACE THE MADNESS

LEAN IN TO THE MADNESS

If you are going to listen to me and embrace a touch of the madness, you must really open up to it, lean in to it, and be it. You can't do something wonderfully crazy and not claim it as your own—the disparity and mixed messages will hurt you.

Imagine being a polite, timid revolutionary: "I'd like to overthrow you, but I don't want to be rude—it's not my thing."

Or a cold polar bear: "Can't we just go south and stay there? Maybe get a condo on the beach?"

Or a vampire who hates the dark: "I'm telling you, Igor, two hundred sunblock would work. Just try!"

Don't be that.

Lean in to the madness, embrace it, be it.

PSYCHOS AT THE POOL

On my first day at my first Cannes Film Festival, I came down from my room at the Majestic Hotel and walked out onto the deck by the pool, overlooking the Mediterranean. Beautiful people everywhere, schmoozing, drinking, gossiping. I'd dreamed about going to Cannes my whole life; I felt such amazement and gratitude for just being there.

My name shouted out in a hoarse New York accent broke my reverie.

"Larry, Larry, how could you do this to me? You hate me! How could you stick me in such an old, run-down place to stay?" yelled Julia Phillips. Julia had produced the movies *Taxi Driver*, *Close Encounters of the Third Kind*, and *The Sting*, the latter for which she became the first woman to win an Academy Award for Best Picture.

We brought her—meaning, arranged and paid for—to Cannes to promote a movie we'd just made with her called *The Beat*. An early attempt at a battle rap film, it was terrible, I think. I like to say it was a precursor to Eminem's movie, *8 Mile*, but in reality, that's probably just what I told myself so I could sleep at night.

Back to Julia, who kept ordering fifty-dollar drinks and charging them to my room.

"Julia," I remember saying, "it's old because we got you an eighteenth-century villa in the hills overlooking the bay. We are in Europe."

Before she could argue back, I noticed she was sitting with my relatively new friends, John and Bo Derek. As you might recall from earlier, we wanted to make with them a sequel to the movie *10*.

John, of course, as much as I liked him, was also complaining about something, and also charging everything to my room. Bo, as usual, was lovely.

And they still looked like a light was shining and the wind was blowing only on them.

Another actress we had also brought stopped by to, as I recall, just kind of reminisce about the world and her many suicide attempts. A few years prior, a famous actor had accused her of stabbing him. Our publicists had forgotten that and, a few weeks earlier, sat them both next to each other at an event of ours.

How they all found each other and figured out they had me in common to complain about, in only one morning, I never figured out.

Five minutes ago, all I could see were the gorgeous movie stars, the beautiful hotel deck, the boats bobbing in the bay, happy to not just be in Cannes, but be a part of it.

Now, I looked around at the cacophony of whines, complaints, self-absorption—not to mention the enormous food and drink bill—and realized: what we have here is a bunch of psychos at the pool.

But then I took a breath and realized these psychos were all or partially responsible for the movies *The Sting*, *Close Encounters*, *10*, *The Ten Commandments*, *Exodus*, *Taxi Driver*, and lots more.

They all had a touch of the madness, some more than others of course, but it was there. Was it worth the whining and the lunch tab? You bet. These psychos at the pool, I further realized, are MY psychos, my new compadres, so time to embrace them.

I've now spent a lifetime having meetings like that with psychos at the pool, and I wouldn't trade it for anything. That, I believe, is embracing the madness.

DON'T LISTEN

You know how everyone tells you to listen, listen, listen? Be a good listener? Well, my advice is to listen less. Sometimes, even, don't listen at all. Because people will try to dissuade you. They want to pull you down more than they want to prop you up. That current of the river of life I mentioned at the beginning will try to pull you to the middle. So don't listen.

The most important words in the universe are the ones you tell yourself. Listen to those.

YOU CAN'T START—HELLO, HELLO???

I was sitting in a fisherman's teak longboat in the Andaman sea off the coast of Krabi about to start the Thailand portion of our shoot for the first *Mortal Kombat* movie when the studio called from LA.

"You know, you are not greenlit to start the shoot yet," the voice from back home said. We had been squabbling about something—I don't even remember what.

I looked around as the fisherman and I bobbed in the surf. Crew, lights, actors, tech people, cameras, all set to start shooting that morning. The LA portion of our shoot had gone great, Thailand was amazing, and I believed with a touch of the madness zeal we had a hit movie on our hands.

So I played the ol' trick you see on sitcoms and bad comedy movies—I made crackling noises, skipped every other word of my sentence: "I . . . hear . . . would . . . to help . . . but . . ." and hung up, pretending a bad connection. It wasn't as cliché then!

And then I did what any decent producer with a touch of the madness would do.

I picked up my megaphone, looked at the cast and crew, and shouted, "Action!"

We started shooting. The studio never even called back. Neither of us mentioned it until, well, now.

Sometimes, just don't listen to any words but your own. Remember, once again, the most important words in the universe are the ones you tell yourself.

The movie went on to be a monster hit.

MAKE ADVERSARIES PARTNERS

Negotiations change as you change depending on how you look at the person across the table. With a touch of the madness, you might look at them differently, to your advantage.

In addition to movies at Vestron, my first job, we made lots of music videos and music-related video content.

Right when I started, Michael Jackson was at his height. He had just made his epic music video for "Thriller." We tried to figure out how to put it on home video, but at only thirteen minutes long, it was too short, we thought in those days, for people to buy or rent as a video.

We hit on the idea to make a documentary, *Making Michael Jackson's Thriller*, which we did with HBO, and also included "Thriller" on it. That way, the audience would pay for one hour of content, including "Thriller," not just the "Thriller" music video.

It worked and became the first million-selling videocassette in history.

So we did more: a double cassette of Elton John called *Night & Day* (The Night Time Concert). We did *Video Rewind* with the Rolling Stones, featuring the band in the future in an attic finding their "old" music videos and rewinding through them; a documentary on the Beach Boys; and more.

They all hit and sold really well. But it occurred to me, what if we could do this same kind of thing for a much older demographic. Music videos for your parents or grandparents.

Madness, I was told, of course.

I persisted. I just had an instinct that demographic, if given the opportunity, would also love music videos. Vestron gave me the green light.

"HEY, KID, YOU DIRECT IT!"

The most famous performer then for the grandparent set was Liberace. The recent subject of an HBO movie, Liberace was an ultra-flamboyant singer and pianist, and reportedly the highest-paid performer in the world in the fifties and sixties. He was still really famous to an older demo in the 1980s.

I set off to Atlantic City, New Jersey, to a casino where Lee, as people called him, was doing a bunch of shows. We had the whole venue during the day to ourselves to shoot what we believed to be the first-ever Liberace music videos.

But the director got caught in traffic on the New Jersey Turnpike and was late.

I tried to stall Lee's manager, who, in my memory of long ago, looked kind of like a cartoon frog with a huge cigar. He could have walked out of vaudeville in the forties.

The manager came out from backstage and walked right up to me, like two inches away. He held up the script I had sent him for the day's shoot.

"Hey, kid, we read your script," he snarled in between cigar puffs.

"Oh, that's great, as soon as the director gets here, we'll—" I tried to say.

He interrupted me.

"Here's what we think of your script, kid." He then raised it to my face, meaning, over his head because he was really short, ripped it into tiny little pieces, and then threw the pieces in the air like confetti.

He blew cigar smoke in my face, said, "We start in five minutes," and turned to go backstage.

"But the director's still not here," I yelled behind him.

He stopped, turned, and said, "Hey, kid, you direct it." Then he went backstage in a puff of smoke.

I have to admit, I kind of liked the little guy.

Anyway, I had no experience as a director. None. Liberace was a legend, and I went out on the line convincing Vestron to try a "grandparent music video" project.

Now I had four minutes. No director. And of course, no script.

I had produced a bunch of music projects, as I mentioned, so I figured I would just have to try to brim with confidence and give it a shot.

But I really had no idea what to do.

You know who did know exactly what to do?

Liberace. He was great. Fabulous. Amazingly professional, kind, humble, and an incredible performer.

As I would try to explain an idea for a shot I had, he knew before I even finished what I was trying to say and performed it better than I even imagined.

The whole day went like that.

Liberace passed away soon after, but our first, and maybe the only, set of Liberace music videos sold incredibly well for years.

The point is, I had taken a shot but almost viewed Lee and his manager as adversaries, in a sense. Could I get them to do X? Will they listen to me about Y? In reality, Lee, and even his manager, wanted nothing more than an amazing result, and when it came to the performance, they were incredible partners and totally gracious.

They were pros, and pros will work with you, even if they do hate your script and blow cigar smoke in your face.

I use that lesson—try to make those across the negotiating table your partners—to this day.

As I am writing this (fall '22), we are finishing a movie unlike most of what I do. This is a fictional film designed to bring awareness to a current humanitarian issue.

To make the movie, I convinced virtually everyone —music composers; sound engineers; editors; my partner, Jimmy; visual effects team; etc.—to work for no money, just for gross points. Everyone said yes. I suppose if you have heard of this movie when you read this, we will have succeeded in the film, but either way, everyone I usually negotiate with became, in effect, partners to make a movie with a purpose.

Next time you negotiate with a vendor, maybe ask yourself if she is more of a partner. It sounds crazy at first, and it is a touch of the madness, but it often works.

GO BIGGER

Often when we face a big creative challenge, which seems daunting and is perhaps not going so well, we tend to retreat. We are told to not bite off more than we can chew, not to have such delusions of grandeur, to try something more our speed, and all these other clichés which wind up influencing us.

I disagree. A touch of the madness tells us in these situations to do the opposite. When the task seems impossible, rather than chunking it down and going smaller, go bigger.

ONE MOVIE IS TOUGH; TWELVE IS EASIER

Several years ago, I had an idea to make a lower budget animated movie, based on a big brand, and raise all the money independently. I couldn't sell it.

So I figured if I couldn't sell one lower budget animated movie, maybe I could sell twelve. That's called a slate—a whole lineup of movies, in this case, all animated, all based on big IP (intellectual property) brands.

I went bigger when logic would dictate to go smaller (or give up), and it worked.

Why?

There is some logic to investors and bankers making more money from a bigger deal, but I don't think that's it.

A touch of the madness tells you to double down on your idea, believe in it no matter what, and go for it.

I think investors, distributors, the press respond to confidence. Not fake confidence—be genuine—but real passion for your creation. I thought this was a great idea.

And we made under this deal the first feature-length Lego movie, *Lego: The Adventures of Clutch Powers*.

So next time you are having trouble selling something, raising money, getting buy-in at work, don't worry—go bigger!

Here's another example.

MORTAL KOMBAT *FLORIDA—FLAWLESS VICTORY!*

We sold a fantasy martial arts TV series based on our *Mortal Kombat* franchise, called *Mortal Kombat Conquest*. I think the budget for twenty-four shows was $24 million (could be off a bit in memory, but I'll use this to illustrate the point).

That is not a lot of money for a series with lots of adventure and great fights. The studio wanted us to go to New Zealand, which is lovely and inexpensive. The problem is that it is far. Here is why that is an issue.

One of my touches of the madness involves fight scenes in movies and TV. I have done hundreds and always want to show an authentic martial artist doing an amazing move. A flurry of kicks and punches wildly edited resulting in someone mysteriously winding up on the ground is the opposite of what I want.

I like to say, "You have never seen the move before, but you actually do SEE someone doing it."

To achieve that, we constantly scour the world for amazing martial artists, aerialists, gymnasts, and fly them in, sometimes for just one shot. It pays off.

You can't do that if you are in New Zealand. It's just too long a flight and too far on a TV production schedule. We were to have three fights per episode, almost unheard of, and a dedicated fight unit shooting the whole time. They needed people who could be flown in and out quickly, often with little notice.

What to do?

I drive studios crazy with this because I think it is what the audience wants. They certainly view it as a touch of the madness (a nice way of saying they think I am crazy in this regard). I explain all this because everything I did, where we shot the show and what I am about to tell you, all derived from my insisting on the absolute best martial artists in the world, even for one shot.

I figured out Orlando, Florida, would be the place to go. I will skip all the production details, but it would work. The problem is, it was about 20 percent more than New Zealand, or $5 million.

The studio gave me a week to make it work or off to New Zealand.

I flew to Orlando and asked everyone—unions, shooting stages, locations, actors, to cut their fees by 20 percent so we could bring the show to Orlando. While warmly open to the idea, no one said yes, and my week was running out.

What to do when no one is saying yes, but I need them to make our 720-degree aerial round kicks better?

Go bigger.

I decided to hold a press conference and invite the entire city—politicians, unions, the press, city officials, theme park execs, actors, crew—everyone.

I told, in effect, the whole city that I had $24 million to bring them, but only if they would all pitch in, and if everyone would cut costs 20 percent. Or else, I would have to take it out of the country.

Now, everybody, in front of each other, changed. The city gave us money. MGM/Disney studios gave us a great deal. We agreed with them, in exchange, our set could be an actual stop on their tour, and Disney guests could watch us shooting from an observation booth. They encouraged us to interact with the guests via a microphone, which I often did, not only to make Disney happy, but because it was fun and therefore made me happy.

The unions were receptive. We realized union members in TV sometimes had a sort of odd economic situation. The union day rates were great, but many only worked a few days a year. So we guaranteed them, I think, thirty weeks a year of work, if they would cut their day rate by 20 percent. Of course, this worked out to be much, much more for them.

My ask was not to one person, but to the whole city. That is what turned the tide.

Go bigger.

"WE MUST THROW A PARTY IN YOUR HONOR"

Shooting a movie in Southern Thailand while staying in a luxury resort on an island just off the beautiful coast of Krabi I think is as near an ideal paradise work situation as you can find. That's how we shot part of the first *Mortal Kombat* movie.

The island, the magical beaches dotted with (rock) outcroppings, warm trade winds, translucent light-green ocean, glimmering white beaches, and the fragrance of local flowers in the air kind of lull you into a state of relaxed, detached, blissful peace.

In this state of semi-nirvana, late one night, I was walking—more floating—across the little island resort to my waterfront bungalow (OK, I'm bragging), not really noticing anything, when I almost tripped on...

A fourteen-foot Burmese python.

First, I know, given the snakes and wizards mentioned in chapter four, I seem to meet a lot of pythons. Not quite sure why this happens, but it does. Honestly, I kind of like them, but not alone, late at night.

Back to the python in my path. And there was only one path. I had no place to go.

He was stretched across the path about one foot from me. It was really late on this small island. No one was around. I had no cell phone. Yelling would have done nothing.

I had no idea what to do, so I did nothing. I just kind of became very still. The python looked at me, deliberately, as if making a decision, like the Terminator did with Axl Rose, and then looked ahead and slowly slithered away. Maybe he was in a state of relaxed nirvana, too.

Finally, he was out of my way and I took off running back to my room.

But this isn't about me. It is about the hotel manager, who I told bright and early the next morning that I almost tripped over a huge python, and that has to be so dangerous, and how can he guarantee my crew would be safe, when he interrupted me.

The hotel manager clapped his hands in utter joy, like I could not have given him better news.

"That is wonderful! The snake you met is the Protector Goddess of the island. Very few people ever see her. This is very lucky for you, very auspicious."

"Um, really, it is?" I asked.

"Oh yes, wonderful. We must throw a party in your honor to celebrate immediately."

"A party, for me? Um, well, that would be fun I guess."

He totally had me.

And the next day, he did throw a lovely party, for me, after we finished shooting, at sunset, with champagne and great food and lots of people, all to celebrate my good fortune in meeting the Protector Goddess of the island. I had a blast.

I never found out if this was the most resourceful hotel manager in the world, who turned a scary wildlife encounter into a party to appease his guest, or if it really was the Protector Goddess of the island.

But either way, talk about going bigger! He could have apologized a hundred times, called snake catchers, offered me a room upgrade, but instead that hotel manager leaned in to a touch of the madness, embraced it, and threw me a huge party. And he made his guest—me—really happy, and I will never forget the story.

NEVER GIVE UP

REALLY.

NEVER, EVER, EVER GIVE UP.

It takes ten years to become an overnight success, my uncle Sam always told me. You just never hear about the first nine and a half.

Perseverance, the courage to continue against all odds, is, in my experience, the single most determinative factor in whose mad idea succeeds and whose does not.

I know I have talked about this earlier in the book, but I am reminding you again because it is so important.

Here is one more example.

ROCK ON

We made a movie at Vestron called *Dream a Little Dream*. It featured Corey Haim and Corey Feldman, two teen actors whose fame in the mid-nineties is hard to describe it was so massive.

The movie was a dreamy, sweet, body-switching film. The director was both a Pied Piper to these kids and others like them (in a good way), and had an out-there, beautiful kind of trippy vision we supported.

That was consistent with my philosophy of betting on the extreme—the madness—and letting them go wild.

What I did not count on here was part of "the wild." Essentially, we had a bunch of kids—actors who were actual kids, and young filmmakers—all making a movie on the beach in North Carolina. And we largely left them alone. Perhaps a slight miscalculation.

Today, we see what is shot on a set almost instantaneously, wherever we are in the world no matter where the set is, because of digital dailies (dailies are the raw footage shot every day). In those days, movies were shot on actual film we shipped across the country, to a lab, which developed it, and booked a screening room in which to show it. Thus, we were always about a week behind if we were not on set.

The last week of shooting, things had been going great. I left to start another movie.

I later learned that, in that last week of shooting, the director had completely changed the script. And to get one of the shots in the new script, they cut down a tree in the center of town, which turned out to be the town's landmark.

The tree aside, the new ending just did not really make sense in my opinion.

Now, I take full responsibility; I backed them, they took a shot, but it doesn't always work. By the time we realized what had happened, the crew was wrapped from North Carolina. Vestron would not pay to send everyone back for reshoots, figuring a movie in those days with Corey and Corey would do well, no matter what.

It opened huge Friday night, but then tanked during the weekend. What to do?

Give up? No way.

Jimmy Ienner (remember, my now partner who godfathered *Dirty Dancing*?) called up and said one of the songs, a cover of a seventies hit called "Rock On," done for our movie by a former soap opera star named Michael Damian, was "getting a lot of heat."

Jimmy said, "Listen, can you make a music video and get it to MTV in like a week?" I said sure, not having any idea how I would.

He said, "Great, I will have the record company (that was doing the soundtrack) release 'Rock On' as a single next week, and we will premiere it on the Billboard 100 chart at, oh, let's see, number twenty-seven."

"Wait, how can you know now what number it will premiere at next week?"

Jimmy laughed and told me to go make the video. Since I had fought so hard to go for reshoots and lost that one, the company agreed to fund the video.

We reassembled the cast and the crew in LA, hired friends, dancers, everyone we could grab, kind of threw a party, shot it with Michael Damian playing, and had our video, just when—

"Rock On" premiered on the charts at number twenty-seven, just like Jimmy said.

He told me, "It's really picking up steam. Get the video to MTV this week. I'll take the song to, let's see, number eleven next week."

"OK, this is crazy, how—" He laughed and hung up again.

We delivered the video to MTV, who agreed to air it (a big deal in those days).

Next week: "Rock On" was number eleven, our video was playing in heavy rotation on MTV, but the movie, theatrically, was over, so to speak. The audience just had too much trouble with the ending.

Jimmy called. "OK, next week we go to number one!"

"Are you ever going to tell me how you are doing this?"

"Probably not."

Next week, we had a hit song, the number one single in the country and a hit video.

This all spurred a "Rock On" tour, which lasted for months, and some say saved the record company. It's my first gold record. The home video sales of the movie were huge. We even made a sequel film.

All from a failed movie that we never gave up on.

By the way, I still don't know how Jimmy did it.

DON'T BE AFRAID

The most repeated phrase in the Bible is "Don't be afraid." And while I doubt it referred to a touch of the madness, you never know . . .

One day, long ago, someone had to suggest this to his tribe. "Hey, you know those disgusting longish red things with the big front claws and bug eyes and tentacles crawling around the bottom of the ocean snarfing up garbage? Let's eat 'em."

Someone else had to go to their king, who could execute you if he didn't like what you were saying, and ask, "So how about giving us a ton of money and a bunch of guys to just hop in some huge boats and go that way (points out to sea) for as long as we can until we find something, or plummet off the edge of the earth."

And you might have an idea that sounds just as out there you are not sharing. Why? What if your idea is as good as lobster or finding America?

Of course, the kids in school might make fun of you—well, not really, presumably you are well out of school. But even if not—so what?

Everyone might just love your crazy idea, which might not be as crazy as you worry.

Don't be afraid of trying your idea. You know the old quote, you miss 100 percent of the shots you don't take.

"THE MORALS OF A GERBIL"

When the internet really started taking off, we launched a company to develop TV ideas online. We figured we'd post a lot of ideas in mini, short-form versions and migrate to TV the ones that worked online. Sounds old but it was a new idea then.

We already had our animation studio at that point and wanted to make an adult animated comedy series, similar in tone to *The Simpsons* or *Family Guy*. I love these shows, but if you don't watch, they really push the boundaries and make fun of sex, religion, families, alcohol, and more. Cartoon characters get away with murder.

So we decided to create a show that parodied something we knew a little about—Hollywood.

The Producer was a workplace comedy whose tagline was something like: "Weasels, Scumbags, and Hookers—Just like Hollywood."

One of the cartoon characters was an agent called "the Blue Jew." Before you get too offended, realize I am Jewish, the show made fun of everyone, and we hoped could do it in an *All in the Family* way. (That was a seminal hit show in the seventies that shed light on prejudice by portraying the main character, Archie Bunker, as a total racist; and it was funny.)

The Blue Jew wore a blue velour running suit, gold chains, and entertained himself by tossing sliced deli meat onto passed-out hookers on his coffee table. The *Washington Post* later wrote, "*The Producer* . . . depicts a Hollywood agent with the morals of a gerbil."

Jerry Springer, of talk show fame, voiced the Blue Jew. Tom Arnold (*True Lies*) voiced the character of the producer. Jaime Pressly (*My Name Is Earl, Mom*) voiced his wild assistant.

It took off and became an early internet hit. *TV Guide* wrote: "Utterly reprehensible . . . and actually pretty funny," which I thought was fair.

All these characters of course we made up. Pure fiction. Not actually based on anybody.

Then a funny thing happened. An agent called, furious. "Kasanoff, you mother"—exactly, by the way, what the Blue Jew always said—"this character is based on me. I'm gonna sue your ass off."

Uh-oh.

But wait, it wasn't based on him.

Then something occurred to me, so I said, "Let me get this straight. You are going to stand up in front of the world and swear on a stack of bibles in a court of law that your favorite hobby is to throw sliced deli meat onto hookers passed out in your living room? That's you? You do that and want the world to know?"

Silence.

Then, "I hate you, Kasanoff." He hung up.

Crisis averted.

But an even funnier thing happened next. More agents and talent managers started calling up, saying, "That's me, right? The Blue Jew is based on me, isn't he?"

But they weren't mad. It seemed like most were happy. Like they wanted the slight brush with fame, even if it meant being associated with a character with the morals of a gerbil.

Had we been afraid of trying this, of such wild characters or getting sued by wannabe Blue Jews or getting nailed by the press, this project would not have been noticed. We couldn't have made the Blue Jew just a little annoying, for example. We had to embrace the madness and go all the way.

Or nothing.

And look at all the agents and managers, crazy as it sounds, who wanted to be him.

Ask yourself if there is something you have always wanted to try, a wild innovation, but you never really mentioned it because you thought it was too crazy. What if your peers don't like it, or your boss, or your board?

So what? Try it anyway.

FIND MADNESS IN OTHERS

As I am writing this, I just closed a deal to help someone I just met—dynamic woman but no prior experience in the film business—with a film she had started, which turned into a bit of a mess.

When we closed, she asked, "Why would you take a chance on me?"

I said, "Easy. You have a touch of the madness."

If you are going to embrace this in yourself, look for it and embrace it in others. I cast movies this way, make deals this way, and take chances on new people like I just did.

How to spot it?

"HEH, HEH, DAT'S FUNNY"

One of my first assignments at Vestron was to go meet *Penthouse* publisher Bob Guccione and make some movies and videos with him. *Penthouse* was a really popular adult magazine in the seventies, eighties, and nineties. We targeted R-rated historical epics for the films.

Mind you, I was an Ivy League kid (Cornell and Wharton), from a wonderful family in Boston, with, at the time, no exposure to people like Bob or things like *Penthouse*.

Austin, my boss, came with me to the first meeting. Having no idea what to expect, we found that Bob lived in one of the largest private houses in Manhattan, two townhouses in fact, that he had joined together on the Upper East Side. Tasteful and gorgeous, marble columns carved by artisans, imported from Italy, adorned the place.

But in the entryway was a fat guy who looked like he walked out of *The Sopranos*, watching cartoons on a little portable TV set, chuckling, blurting out, "Heh, heh, dat's funny!"

Oh, and he had a revolver stuck in his belt.

While waiting, occasionally doors would open where you don't think there would be doors—hidden in the walls—and either models would come out, giggling, then disappear down the hall into other hidden doors, or Dobermans would come out and roam around.

But again, magnificent art hung on the walls. He owned paintings by Matisse, Botticelli, Chagall, Renoir, Picasso, Van Gogh, and more.

Copies of *Penthouse* magazines lay on the coffee table in the waiting area. Quite, um, extreme. Almost hard-core.

But again, he also published *Omni* magazine, about science. He gave money every year to nuclear-fusion clean-energy research. Brandeis honored him for his "editorial attention to critical issues of the day."

Finally, an assistant ushered us into the conference room to meet Bob and one of his business advisors. Bob wore a bright yellow silk shirt, almost all unbuttoned, with a gold chain. If the guy with the gun at the door laughing at the cartoons looked like he came from *The Sopranos*, Bob looked like he had walked straight out of a scene from *The Godfather*, maybe having been smoking cigars with Marlon Brando.

His advisor, as I recall, was a smart, successful, accomplished New York rainmaker type.

We sat down to talk. Austin said, "Bob, we want to make three movies you produce; kind of R-rated historical epics, and we'll pay ten million dollars per movie."

Then, the advisor turned to Bob and said, "Bob, they want to make three movies you produce; kind of R-rated historical epics, and they'll pay ten million dollars per movie."

No kidding. Austin and I tried not to look at each other.

Bob said, "Can I have script approval?"

The advisor said, "Can Bob have script approval?"

Mind you, we were all speaking English.

Austin said, "OK, but we want director approval."

The advisor said, "OK, but they want director approval."

The whole meeting went on like this.

Say you, reading this, run R & D for a Fortune 500 company, or head up marketing for a tech start-up. You might be thinking, *Entertaining, but what does this story have to do with me?*

Here's what.

My monk friend, Thich Nhat Hanh, had a great expression: Be still and know.

I learned then, with Austin's help, to look beyond the exterior madness. The guy with the gun, the dogs from hidden doors, the English-to-English translation—maybe they were a game, maybe an actual ton, not touch, of the madness.

And yes, he was a complete dichotomy and fascinating, but if you became still, and let all those things roll off your back, you realized he was, above all, passionate to an extreme about his beliefs.

Here is why that realization was important. Almost no one invests in their own movie. Or video. If the studio gives you $10 million, you spend ten, maybe ask for more, but never spend your own money.

Bob would, we reasoned. He would spend whatever it took beyond what we gave him to realize his vision, creatively and artistically.

So that meant, if we were willing to overlook the superficial eccentricities, which were irrelevant, it turned out, his real touch of the madness, his artistic passion, would mean we would pay for a $10 million movie, but for example get a $20 million one.

And that is exactly what happened (numbers not exact) on the projects we did together.

So no matter who you are or what your job is, learn to look beyond the exterior madness, be still, and know the deep-down one. A touch of the madness is not about, say, wearing funny hats. It's about what goes on in the head of the guy underneath the hat. Then decide if that touch of the madness works for you or not.

A TOUCH OF THE MADNESS AT HOME

The purpose of this book is to hopefully get you to embrace your inner madness in your professional life so you can be optimally innovative and creative.

But it does work in all aspects of your life if you want it to. While my goal is not to be intrusive personally, it is worth a minute because the more you adopt this as a lifestyle, as a reflex almost, the better it will work professionally.

No long stories, but personally, I have embraced a touch of the madness in:

- Travel: Most Christmas vacations I plan three days ahead; for a recent one, I had a whim that it would be fun to travel around Italy, meeting different artists, spending the day in their studios, seeing how they work, and learning from them. Every concierge at hotels around Italy we called to help said they had never been asked that question (ASK), and they all helped. And with only a few days of planning, I took oil painting in Venice; sketching in Florence; fresco painting on the banks of the Arno River, also in Florence; and ceramics in Sienna. I tell you this not to brag about my vacations, because the only thing I did most others don't is to ask.

- Hobbies: I love photography and elephants, so in my spare time over the last five years, I shot a photo coffee-table book with all the proceeds going to charity and am trying to sell it now; I have no prior experience with coffee-table books or helping elephants, but so what?
- Relationships: Well, trust me, a touch of the madness doesn't even begin to cover it.

You get the point.

With what is comfortable for you, if you want, you can use the principles in this book across your whole life, and if you do, they will improve your effectiveness in your professional life.

THE MADNESS AND MINDFULNESS

There is a French film from the sixties called *The King of Hearts*. Here's the story.

During World War II, villagers in rural France quickly abandon their town, running from the Nazis. But they forget about everyone in the town's insane asylum. A Scottish soldier, separated from his unit, poses as one of the inmates just ahead of the Nazis' arrival. When the Nazis move on, satisfied only the insane people are left, they leave the gates to the asylum open.

The inmates now playfully run the town. They think the Scotsman is their king. He keeps trying to tell them there is a bomb hidden in the town and they have to find it before it explodes. They keep enjoying freedom, flowers, the river, each other, games, and dancing.

Towards the end, when the Scotsman has fallen in love with the beautiful, ethereal, dancing inmate played by Geneviève Bujold, and the British and Germans are attacking outside, and the bomb is about to explode, he looks at her, lovingly, and says:

"There are three minutes left to live."

She replies: "Three minutes is great!"

This film is a terrific study in mindfulness and madness.

The theme: who is crazy—the "sane people" killing each other or the inmates living only in the moment?

I'm a proponent of doing everything mindfully, but this book isn't really a primer on mindfulness. As it relates to a touch of the madness, however, the dancing inmate has the right attitude.

So much of what I am encouraging you to do—create, ask anyone anything, never give up your dreams, play—simply works better if you do it one thing at a time, enjoying the present moment and the fact you are pursuing ultimate creativity and innovation.

As my old friend Thay says, "When you drink your tea, you drink your tea. That is mindfulness of drinking tea."

If we never got the shot on the Aman yacht, I still spent three days on a great yacht in a magical setting. But I was so present and relaxed, I got better shots. See?

Here is the difference in my life at the Cannes Film Festival before and after I discovered mindfulness. At Cannes, people yell, scream, negotiate, worry, don't treat the poor waiters well, stress about invitations to the right parties.

I hate to admit, but I was probably guilty of some of that early on.

After mindfulness, I was on a yacht in the harbor talking about a movie, and everyone, of course, was screaming. I actually said, not that I am a guru or anything, "Look where we are? We're on a yacht in one of the prettiest places in the world, talking about making a movie, our dream. Enjoy it. Relax." I still negotiated hard but much more mindfully. We resolved everything.

Here is an example of how applying mindfulness to a touch of the madness worked with an actual group of Buddhist monks.

THAY IN THAILAND

I mentioned earlier how I met Zen master/Buddhist monk Thich Nhat Hanh, who everyone called Thay, which is Vietnamese for "teacher." And how he asked me to make a documentary on mindfulness, which I did.

Before I finished the documentary and was able to show it to Thay, he had a stroke. He survived years longer than doctors predicted but was not able to speak.

After I finished, I learned he was recuperating in Thailand. I wasn't sure where, or if I could even find him (the information flow was not great from the monks about this), let alone see him (he saw few people then), but I really wanted to show him, from me, that I did what he asked, and we had this part of his teachings down on film for posterity.

Without a specific location from the monks taking care of him, or confirmation I could see Thay, I went to Thailand to try.

I was based in Bangkok, and each day I got a little closer to finding out where he was and a time I might—might—be able to see him. The other monks told me some days he was up to a visitor, some days not. I could travel all the way there to no avail.

Finally, with maybe a fifty-fifty shot I would get to see Thay, I hired a guide and driver and set off. It took us six hours to find the mountain where we thought he was. It seemed like an old movie, setting off to find the Zen master on a mountaintop in the middle of a Southeast Asian jungle.

After losing our way many times, and the guide wanting to go back, and the cell phones not working, we found him and the monks.

I did get to see him. They wheeled him out, and he sat next to me. He held my hand—half his body had been paralyzed, the other half not. We watched about ten minutes of the documentary until he tired, squeezed my hand again, looked at me lovingly, and was taken away, to rest.

It was the last time I saw him, which I knew it would be. He passed away this year.

Now here is the mindfulness part. Going to see Thay to show him a movie about his mindfulness teachings, one simply has to be mindful!

So, even with all the uncertainty, I didn't worry about finding him or not. I knew I would—I felt I would—but if not, each day in Bangkok, after trying to plan how to get to Thay's, I toured the city, visited temples, saw art, ate at great restaurants, took a boat ride on the river. All peacefully, all mindfully.

When traipsing through the jungle, with the guide panicking, I did not. The jungle was beautiful. One time Thay and I did an interview for the *LA Times* together. Towards the end, the reporter asked Thay if he had anything else to add.

"Look how beautiful the flowers are today," he said. I remembered that, winding through the jungle, looking at the flowers and trees.

Before Thay died, one of the monks, Sister Dang Nghiem, told me Thay had manifested in me everything I needed to learn from him. I felt, after seeing him one last time, holding his hand and showing him we did what he asked, that was true.

Even beyond this, about death, Thay would say a wave is something before it is a wave, it is something after the wave crashes. It changes form but does not go away. There is no birth; there is no death; there is no fear.

"A cloud never dies," Thay would say.

This attitude stayed with me the whole time on my journey to see him. Before going that day, I went on a morning adventure to shoot stills of Khmer ruins (as mentioned, photography is a huge passion of mine).

After seeing him, I returned to Bangkok around 10 PM, and went out to clubs. And I partied all night.

I have told a lot of people about this day—photos in the morning; showing Thay the film the last time I ever saw him; partying late at night.

Some express a kind of shock that I could enjoy the morning and party that night. You know who I think would have loved my doing that?

Thay!

In the morning, it was too early to go. Why not mindfully experience beautiful ancient Khmer ruins, which I love? I even asked the guide to leave me alone so I could just shoot and breathe and be.

And after I saw Thay, I felt great. Why not enjoy the nightlife of Thailand? That is all I did that night; I did it mindfully.

With mindfulness you can do one hundred things a day, as long as you do them one at time, in the present.

I had one of the best days of my life, not just because of the experience with Thay, but because of how mindful I was all day.

It comes down to this: Is it too much of the madness going to Thailand to maybe, possibly, see a monk and maybe, but probably not, show him the film I could have sent?

Not mindfully, yes, it would have been too risky, too uncertain, too expensive, and too anxiety provoking.

Mindfully, it was, as I said, one of the best days, trips, and experiences of my life.

I stand by everything in this book, but I want to add, as I encourage you to embrace a touch of the madness: embrace it with mindfulness, and it will work better, and you will enjoy it more.

Chapter Seven

WRAP

SIDNEY MEETS GOD

Sidney dies and goes to heaven. God greets him and says, "Sid, I'm a little disappointed in you."

Sidney says, "I know, I know. I should have been more of a leader, like Moses. I let my cousin Irving run the deli into the ground. Moses wouldn't have done that. I could have led. Moses would have taken us out of Queens into Brooklyn before the gentrification. We would have been rich!"

God says, "No, I'm not disappointed because you weren't more like Moses."

"Oh, I know. Solomon, I should have been more like Solomon. What was I thinking doing summer stock year-round instead of college? Solomon would have taken the scholarship to SUNY Binghamton and gotten a degree in accounting. I should have been wise like Solomon."

"Wrong again, Sid. No problem not being more like Solomon."

Sidney is getting stumped.

"Wait a minute, I know—Isaac—that guy had faith. When my wife said the whole naked thing at the reunion with her distant cousins from Scotland was a misunderstanding, I should have had faith. I should have been more like Isaac."

God sighs. "Sidney, I'm not disappointed you weren't more like Moses, or Solomon, or Isaac."

"What then? What could it be?" implores poor Sidney.

"Sidney, I'm disappointed you weren't more like Sidney."

This whole book is about embracing a touch of the madness to capture real creativity and innovation. And I stand by it.

But it is also about being yourself. You have to find your level of comfort with all this. You must be authentic. Unlike Sidney, you must embrace a touch of the madness that is right for you, when being 100 percent yourself.

So please:

- Create great ideas that seem impossible— "only the impossible is worth doing."

- Ask anyone you need to help you no matter how insane it sounds; never, ever, ever, give up on them—hold on with a perseverance that seems mad.
- Play! Have a wild fun time doing it all. Make this your state of mind. Don't underrate play and fun. It's important.

Relish when they call you crazy. My sister-in-law thought I was crazy for at least the first ten years she was married to my brother. Half my family does; lots of my friends do, too.

So what? I think it's a compliment.

I am now at the point if people tell me an idea I have for a movie or theme park ride is just great and a slam-dunk, I get a bit nervous. On the other hand, if they tell me I'm crazy and it will never work, the warm glow of giving in to a touch of the madness envelops me like early morning mist on the beach, and I set off to make it.

CREATE; ASK; PLAY.

And do it all with a touch of the madness.

If you do, it will change your life.

THANKS

Thanks to my brother, Bruce, a great and successful writer of books, newsletters, posts, and insights, and a top coach to thought leaders and CEOs, for his help and advice and, of course, for putting up with my madness all these years with great equanimity.

Thanks to Jimmy Ienner, my partner, friend, and adopted godfather, for his guru-like guidance through the maze of the madness.

Thanks to Jim George, stillness coach extraordinaire, for his support and help in matters both practical and more, well, deep.

Thanks to my awesome agent, Bill Gladstone of Waterside, and wonderful publisher, Glenn Yeffeth of BenBella Books. I decided I wanted to write this book one day in the fall of '22, and a mutual acquaintance introduced me to Bill over the phone. We spoke on a Monday, hit it off right away. I pitched him the idea and sent him the book proposal. The next day, he was my agent and had a great idea about who should publish it.

Bill sent it to Glenn, his old friend and colleague, that same Tuesday. Wednesday, the three of us Zoomed and again got along great—these are fun guys. Thursday, Glenn made a proposal, and Friday, we had a deal.

I never spoke to any other agent or publisher. Know why? It was so obvious these guys have themselves a touch of the madness, so who better than them?

And a publisher with a touch of the madness, if my theory is correct, should have a team who is also wonderfully creative and open-minded and, yes, a bit mad. And they do! I want to thank my wonderful editor, Leah Wilson, and our "can't believe he finds all these ways to make this better" copy editor, Scott Calamar. In fact, the whole BenBella team is terrific!

Thanks to my ol' pal Pam Meyer, author of the hit book *Liespotting*, great speaker (huge TED Talk), and, as it turns out, wise counselor, for her advice and support.

Thanks to Zanzibar the Treasure Hunting Dog, whose editorial notes were slim but whose moral support as he sat with me during the entire writing of this book was invaluable.

Mostly I want to thank all the great scoundrels, psychos, weasels, artists, Buddhist monks, *Playboy* models, eccentric actors, cartoon characters, passionate directors, and slippery studio execs who make up the cast of all the true stories in this book.

One quick note about the stories. They are all, to the best of my recollection, true. Sometimes I changed the names in case the people mentioned, or their heirs, want anonymity. I am sure some of the details—exact dates, numbers attached to deals, the exact way someone said something—might be a little off as filtered through the haze of memory. But even if so, the point of them remains solid.

ABOUT THE AUTHOR

 Larry Kasanoff is chairman/CEO of Threshold Entertainment Group. Threshold makes movies, animated movies, and location-based entertainment largely based on some of the world's biggest brands, including Spider-Man, Mortal Kombat, Justice League, Lego, Star Trek, Marvel, and Star Wars.

Larry is the producer or executive producer of Mortal Kombat media, including three number-one films, a television series, an animated series, platinum-selling soundtracks, and a live tour.

He is the executive producer of the box-office smash film *True Lies*, starring Arnold Schwarzenegger and directed by James Cameron.

Previously, as president and cofounder of Lightstorm Entertainment, Larry supervised production, marketing, publicity, and merchandising for the four-time Academy Award–winning hit *Terminator 2: Judgment Day*, directed by James Cameron.

He produced two movies with Academy Award–winning director Kathryn Bigelow.

As a producer or studio head, Larry has made over two hundred feature films, including *Dirty Dancing* and the Academy Award winner for Best Picture *Platoon*. He has raised well over a billion dollars in the film business.

He has made theme park rides, including Marvel Superheroes 4D, The Amazing Adventures of Spiderman, and Star Trek: The Borg Adventure.

In the music world, Larry has packaged or produced video projects with several of the world's biggest talents, including Michael Jackson, the Rolling Stones, and Dick Clark. For *Terminator 2*, he produced MTV's top video of the year, "You Could Be Mine" with Guns N' Roses.

Threshold and/or Larry has been profiled in the *New York Times*, the *Wall Street Journal*, *USA Today*, *Time* magazine, *Wired*, and *Maxim* and has been featured on CNN, Fox News, *ABC World News Tonight*, CNBC, *The Howard Stern Show*, and more.

Larry holds an MBA from the Wharton School of Business and a BA from Cornell University.